Studies in Childhood and Youth

Series editors
Penny Curtis
University of Sheffield
Sheffield, UK

Spyros Spyrou
European University Cyprus
Nicosia, Cyprus

Nigel Thomas
Department of Social Work
University of Central Lancashire
Preston, UK

Afua Twum-Danso Imoh
Department of Sociological Studies
University of Sheffield, UK

This well-established series embraces global and multi disciplinary scholarship on childhood and youth as social, historical, cultural and material phenomena. With the rapid expansion of childhood and youth studies in recent decades, the series encourages diverse and emerging theoretical and methodological approaches. We welcome proposals which explore the diversities and complexities of children's and young people's lives and which address gaps in the current literature relating to childhoods and youth in space, place and time.

Studies in Childhood and Youth will be of interest to students and scholars in a range of areas, including Childhood Studies, Youth Studies, Sociology, Anthropology, Geography, Politics, Psychology, Education, Health, Social Work and Social Policy.

More information about this series at
http://www.springer.com/series/14474

Sarah Coombs

Young People's Perspectives on End-of-Life

Death, Culture and the Everyday

Sarah Coombs
University Campus Suffolk
Ipswich, UK

Studies in Childhood and Youth
ISBN 978-3-319-53630-9   ISBN 978-3-319-53631-6   (eBook)
DOI 10.1007/978-3-319-53631-6

Library of Congress Control Number: 2017939923

Cover credit: Vincent O'Byrne / Alamy Stock Photo

Printed on acid-free paper

This Palgrave Macmillan imprint is published by Springer Nature
The registered company is Springer International Publishing AG
The registered company address is: Gewerbestrasse 11, 6330 Cham, Switzerland

To Paul, Alice, Freddie and Martha

Acknowledgements

Thanks to all those who shared death stuff and death stories.

Contents

1

'It Would Be Better to Talk About Death'

A number of years ago I attended a conference that explored and examined multiple perspectives on the end-of-life. The first speaker, after giving a lively and engaging presentation, firmly concluded that death is a topic for everyone. This was greeted by nods of approval and sustained applause. The next few days provided a rich kaleidoscope of views, with each speaker deftly linking and reinforcing the idea that death was indeed a subject for all. Notwithstanding such vehement protestation, 'all' it would seem, did not include children. Such characters were left unmentioned until the closing stages of the third and final afternoon when most people had packed their bags and were making a hasty retreat to the airport.

Putting aside, for a moment, the assertions and curiosity of death scholars, mortality is perhaps something that we, as adults, might not want to think or talk about too often, although we may lay claim to a mature and sophisticated understanding of it. In particular, we might find discussing the end-of-life with those most engaged in the start of their own to be challenging. Death, in the context of youth, faces adults with a conundrum, which leads to an often elusive but nonetheless effective sidestepping of the issue. Perhaps, adults prefer to keep the

© The Author(s) 2017
S. Coombs, *Young People's Perspectives on End-of-Life*,
Studies in Childhood and Youth, DOI 10.1007/978-3-319-53631-6_1

lid firmly on this particular Pandora's Box for fear of the as yet unde-termined but possibly devastating consequences to both themselves and those deemed too young to face this shocking reality. And yet, if as proposed above, death is indeed a topic for everyone then it must also include the young.

Kastenbaum and Fox suggest that since the end of World War II dominant adult assumptions have been that 'Children do not think about death. Children cannot think about death. Children should not think about death' (2007: 123). I was, and still remain, unconvinced by this argument. Therefore, as these assertions gradually settled into my thoughts, I began to question not only if, as I was sure they did, but how, when and in what ways young-people might indeed think, talk-about and encounter death in their everyday lives. Furthermore, how might I find out? This book represents a voyage of discovery for both myself and the young-people who took part. It illuminates the some-times strange and sad but often funny and enchantingly intricate worlds of death that these young-people inhabit. The text is not positioned as a 'how too' guide, or situated to make audacious claims but rather to shed light on a shared venture into unknown territory. It is perhaps a path less trodden but one well worth the journey.

It may be useful at this point to indicate that I use the terms 'chil-dren' and more often 'young-people' synonymously throughout the book. Not merely as an indication of age but to promote personhood and youth as positive attributes. Definitions of the term 'young', list among its many qualities, youthfulness, freshness, vigour, newness and spirit, all of which, I suggest, provide valuable opportunities for fresh and novel end-of-life perspectives to be aired and shared. At the same time, and in accordance with the United Nations Convention on the Rights of the Child (UNCRC 1989), all the young-people mentioned in this book are deemed to be children by rite of their chronological age. The younger ones may more readily be seen as children and the older ones as in the process of leaving childhood behind. However, their situations within the boundaries of childhood are accompanied by notions of immaturity, futurity, incompetence and innocence, which emphasise the deeply embedded dichotomies between adult and child. Notwithstanding such notions, Gallacher and Gallagher (2008) propose a greater equality, in which all ages grow, develop, mature and become competent together, thereby situating younger and older people on a more even footing. Such ideas usually take time to gather momentum and therefore in relation to youth and death cannot, I suggest, come soon enough.

The chapters that follow bring together the voices of 29 UK based young-people, all aged between 10 and 17 years, who volunteered to explore and share their death related thoughts, feelings and experiences. What becomes clear is that death, for them, is not the 'undiscovered country', famously suggested by Shakespeare's Hamlet, but rather on the contrary, one that is extremely familiar. Consequently, dominant ideologies, which suggest young-people should not be exposed to death or think about its consequences, are frequently challenged.

Without any doubt, I am deeply indebted to these young-people, not only for their keen engagement in the conversations that follow and their frank and forthright discussions but also for allowing me a glimpse into their unique and candid domains of death. I hope that you, the reader, will enjoy visiting these surroundings and some largely hidden aspects of children's lives.

Opening Conversations

> **Justine** [aged 11]: I think if children talked more about it [death], it would be better, because if someone dies that you know you're going to be really upset, and if you've never talked about it, it would be harder for you
>
> **Lottie** [aged 10]: Yeah, because you can talk about death as a celebration of life, and talk about life and death together. They tell children all about life and how you are born but not about dying. It would be better to talk about death

Just as Justine and Lottie contend that talking about death is 'better' than not talking about it, so societies and individuals have pondered their own mortality and all manner of questions pertaining to it. The work of authors, scientists, artists, philosophers and academics attest to the importance of this topic, attempting on humanity's behalf, to explore and uncover the possible truths, meanings and practicalities of death. Famously, Shakespeare's Hamlet begs us to consider this existential uncertainty in the soliloquy, 'To be or not to be'. D.H. Lawrence enquires if we have 'built [y]our ship of death', encouraging us to do so, as 'we will need it' (The Ship of Death 1929/30). T.S. Elliot suggests, 'In my beginning is my end' (East Coker 1940), and Dylan Thomas' (1951) urges us to 'not go gentle into that good night'. Equally, fine art has provided images through which mortality can be glimpsed: the deaths of Marat (Jacques-Louis David 1793), Ophelia (John Everett Millais 1851–1852), Chatterton (Henry Wallis 1856) and The Execution of Lady Jane Grey (Paul Delaroche 1883). Ancient philosophers have mused over our non-existence and more contemporary scholars have questioned if life is to be understood as 'a deliberate, continual turning away from death' (Seale 1998: 11); 'What is it like to die' (Kellehear 2009: xxii); and how does 'death manifest itself within the Western social world' (Hockey et al. 2010: 1). As successive versions of the burial and funeral service in the Anglican Book of Common Prayer confidently articulate, 'In the midst of life we are in death', and that 'Man that is born of a woman hath but a short time to live'.

In the UK today, it can be argued that human exposure to death is ubiquitous, both in the public and the private sphere. Images of death on the TV news, in newspapers and on YouTube permeate our awareness. Internet forums for the bereaved bare testimony to the chatter and our homes provide space for treasured photographs and mementoes of deceased loved ones. Industries pertaining to death take us on trips to Holocaust sites, war graves and the memorials of the rich and famous. National acts of remembrance are performed before mass audiences and popular soap operas relay the deaths and funerals of their central characters to millions of viewers, often resplendent with horse drawn funeral hearse and floral tributes. Within this cacophony of continuous verbal and visual noise the phrase 'as silent as the grave' seems somewhat problematic, and Shakespeare's Macbeth potentially strikes a louder and clearer chord with death as 'full of sound and fury'.

Notwithstanding the above representations and the enduring presence of death in Western media culture, death itself is a continually changing phenomenon, viewed alternately as taboo (Gorer1955, 1965), denied (Becker 1973) and sequestered (Mellor and Shilling 1993). Such positions highlight the potentially invisible nature of personal and actual deaths, in the words of Berridge 'the kind most people die' (2002: 6). However, speaking more generally Kellehear notes, that in the context of death and grief, 'change is afoot' (2007: 73). Walter, in his book of the same title, points to *The Revival of Death* (1994), and Lee goes so far as to suggest that the last two decades have placed death 'at the centre stage of life' (2008: 746). Clearly then, death is a pervasive and changing part of human existence, available to all through a variety of words, images, personal experiences and public performances. The body of work, mentioned above, attests to this fluidity and yet the perspectives and experiences of adults remain the dominant views in the construction and interpretation of death in society. This book therefore, proposes that the time is right to ask what we know about the everyday death-worlds of young-people, to bring their voices to the forefront of end-of-life discussions and challenge the silence attributed to them, [imposed upon them], on this topic.

Thirty years prior to this study, Elias (1985) argued that concealing death from children was firmly established in Western society. More recently, Fearnley (2012) contends that despite many advancements made in relation to children's everyday lives over the last decade, these are not mirrored in relation to dying and death, as adults continue to shield and silence children from engaging in this reality. Faulkner's argument, that contemporary Western societies position the child as a sacred symbol that 'sanctifies' (2011: 105) our very way of life, uncovers just some of the difficulties that adults have in situating death and youth together. Locating death in opposition to an Apollonian vision of childhood, as insidious, contaminating and a threat to youthful innocence and futurity, only compounds the situation further, creating a potential taboo. McManus, drawing on the work of Douglas (1966), proposes that 'the purpose of a taboo is to maintain the boundary between the sacred and the profane' (2013: 10). This book therefore, examines the nature and extent of this boundary and the margins to which both death and childhood have been consigned. It questions if the somewhat uneasy association between death and childhood is indeed the last taboo.

Certainly, within Western societies, it is clear that death is generally considered off-limits, a somewhat malevolent force from which young-people need protection by adults. Silverman identifies this strange paradox, in which Western societies are surrounded by death but 'believe that if we do not talk with children about death, it will not touch them', and therefore we 'protect and insulate them from this fact of life (2000: 2). That the young need shielding from a string of supposedly 'adult only' themes has a long history, Fisher suggesting that 'the two things we keep most secret from our children are birth and death' (2009: 7). Whilst a proliferation of media representations attest to young-people's everyday encounters with death, adults continue to hesitate in engaging with them in these conversations. Such contradictions I argue, lead adults and young-people to an impasse, a suppression of direct dialogue and therefore, silence. Yet, despite this, young-people and death can be seen to share remarkable similarities, both being subject to marginalisation, sequestration, otherness, romanticism, and emotionality rather than reason. They are perhaps more alike than previously realised, and if viewed together can usher in new and exciting perspectives on death. Listening to young-people can provide innovative and creative ways of interacting with age-old questions of mortality. Views and stories that have previously remained private, limited and untold can be re-cast as authoritative voices that can 'open a door to the next world' (Frank 2010: 46).

And yet, despite the marginalisation of death and childhood within the realms of interpersonal communication and academic literature, places have been found for them. Such spaces, in which death and childhood can be viewed together, are more limited and most prominently occupied by research from within the field of developmental psychology. Hunter and Smith (2008), in reviewing literature from the 1940s onwards, point to a concentration of work on children's conceptual understanding of death. Identified as irreversibility, nonfunctionality and universality, it is argued that these develop over time, and are influenced by age, cognitive ability and experience of death, leading to a 'well developed' and 'mature' concept of death around the age of 9 to 10 years. These are not the only spaces in which death and childhood have been explored; consider the seminal work of Bluebond-Langer

(1978) in examining the experiences of dying children, the work of Ribbens McCarthy (2006) with bereaved teenagers and more recently the work of Fearnley (2012) in communicating with children about dying parents. The trajectory of this book hopes to carry on these remarkable conversations but shifts the focus from those of dying children or children with dying parents to young-people's encounters with death in the everyday moment. Despite the purposeful ordinariness of this research encounter and its efforts to discuss end-of-life within the commonplace, the following accounts are remarkable, even extraordinary. From the highly emotive and personal to an 'impersonal distance' (Silverman 2000: 3), we cannot be indifferent to the perspectives of young-people and privilege only the adult voice.

Young-people, so often seen as one homogenous group, marginalised, hidden from view and silenced are now being heard on a number of issues that affect their daily lives and death, I suggest, should be one such topic. In support of research that listens to young-people, I argue that the dominant voices of adults have left young-people's views unheard, their voices subsumed by a grown-up world of death from which they are excluded. Ironically, adults both ignore young-people's views on death, since the topic is considered inappropriate for them, and yet conversely suggest 'a duty to educate' them about it (Beit-Hallahmi 2011: 41), in a similar way to sex education. Neither approach allows the voices of those concerned to be heard. It is as if young-people are a different species, devoid of understanding and emotion, and therefore unable, unless supported by adults, to understand the complexity of human mortality. Wall highlights that children's views actually 'expand what it means to be human' going 'beyond the white noise of adult-centrism' (2010: 3). If by 'white noise' Wall alludes to an all-pervasive sound that drowns out everything else then we need to listen more closely to the complex sound, which echoes the contemporary context of death in the lives of young-people and their unique responses to it.

The aim of the research presented in this book was to bring together the two seemingly disparate and oppositional domains of childhood and death. By combining youthful knowledge, understanding and experience with, among others things, established historical, philosophical, scientific, literary and religious discourses, I hoped to reveal an emergent and everyday picture, illustrating the many ways in which young-people can and do explore and interact with the multifaceted landscapes of death available to them.

Collecting Conversations

Having brought various discourses surrounding death and youth to the table the book will move on to consider ways in which young-people's conversations might be gathered and heard. Kemp (2014) suggests that encounters with death are amongst the most powerful, sensitive and intimate experiences we have. Therefore, despite my own personal convictions that end-of-life should be discussed more often, openly and freely, the way in which this might be done requires thought, planning and reflection. Notwithstanding such deliberation, I believe it is possible to argue that who you are in everyday life is often mirrored by the approach taken to research, and therefore, for me, a qualitative and participant-led approach, based on relationships and care, offered the best possibilities. This 'style', influenced by, amongst others, the paradigm of the New Sociology of Childhood (1997), situates young-people as competent and active social agents, who have rights to participation in society and have their voices heard on subjects pertaining to them. Uprichard argues, that despite the growing increase in research that supports this belief, there is a discrepancy between young-people being conceptualised in this way and the 'type of research they are typically involved in' (2010: 3). She maintains that it is equally important to involve children in research that goes 'beyond childhood' (2010: 3). In line with this, it is perhaps not too bold-a-claim to suggest that this topic is situated beyond the usual remit of childhood research, and to quote my Ph.D. supervisor, 'it's not every day that someone walks into your office and suggests they want to talk to children about death'. Death, as suggested previously, is most commonly viewed as the antithesis of childhood; youth being situated at the start of life, promising bright futures and possibilities, whereas death is viewed as a closing, a degeneration, an end [even if further life is promised beyond]. However, if humanity hopes to understand death and the social world it inhabits, we need to incorporate a variety of views and opinions, and that includes those of children.

Furthermore, both Plummer's discussion of 'critical humanism' (2001) and feminist epistemologies, which promote the virtue of 'care' (Tronto [1993] 2009), helped to build the methodological values and practical principles upon which these conversations could take place. These will be reviewed in greater detail in Chap. 2 but by way of a short introduction, Plummer (2001) implores the social sciences to draw upon their humanistic foundations 'to foster styles of thinking that encourage the creative, interpretive story telling of lives' (2001: 1). This line of thinking encouraged me to utilise the rich cultural and personal resources of these young-people via the collection of everyday household objects, which evoked death for them. Personal artefacts were placed in shoeboxes and brought along to small discussion groups. I refer to this gathering of materials as collecting 'stuff in a box'.

Further qualities of humanistic research of this type are that it is, 'unique, idiographic and human-centred' in its focus, 'relativist' in its epistemology, 'soft', 'warm', 'rich', 'real' and 'personal' in its style, 'inductive' in its theory and 'egalitarian' in its values (Plummer 2001: 9). Attributes which, I suggest, are well-suited to discussing end-of-life issues with anyone, not just the young. My aim therefore, was to engender a caring environment in which ideas, feelings and responses could be heard, shared and reflected upon in reciprocal ways, as demonstrated within feminist ethical approaches. Cockburn argues that feminist methodologies are relational, comparing them to the 'nurturing and dependence' of the mother/child relationship, and emphasising a moral repertoire of 'co-operation, intimacy, trust, connection and compassion' (2005: 78). Although the idealised image of the mother and child can be and often is contested, Cockburn's principles of moral engagement were central to enabling a respectful and relational discourse to emerge within a topic that is frequently positioned as 'sensitive' (Lee 1993; Dickson-Swift et al. 2008). Thereby, young-people's views were promoted to the forefront of these discussions.

I might be accused of over-complicating or over-theorising my approach to what, in essence, were just conversations between friends but for my own sake and more especially for the youthful participants

I felt that firm foundations and solid underpinnings were better to build upon than shifting sand. However, in assuming that young-people have their own views on this topic, and attempting to uncover what these are, is to enter a complex world in which the combination of youthfulness and the end-of-life is seen as paradoxical, or as previously argued, more sensitive than many other areas of social research. Woodthorpe acknowledges, that the study of death has been and remains marginalised within the world of academia or treated with 'morbid fascination' (2008: 30), which in the words of Hockey, is studied by 'at best ... sad down-beat individuals, at worst voyeurs of the macabre' (2007: 436). These unfortunate boundaries that situate death on the periphery of academic research also apply remarkably well to the study of childhood. Arguably, research situated within the context of one of these areas might be viewed as unfortunate, within both, potentially disastrous.

Structuring Conversations

This first chapter has identified key debates that will continue throughout the book. The sociologies of death and of childhood provide a sound base from which to explore the position of death in the lives of young-people. Adult assumptions, and reticence to discuss everyday aspects of the end-of-life with the young have led to a void, which is long overdue a visit. The chapters that follow further elaborate these discussions but unreservedly and wholeheartedly give prominence to the conversations of young-people, as they literally, materially and metaphorically let/get death out of the box.

Chapter 2 discusses changing societal attitudes towards both death and childhood whilst reflecting upon the meanings behind their sometimes oppositional status. Shifting attitudes towards death take centre stage, pitched variously as taboo and sequestered, removed from the public sphere and re-positioned in the realm of the private, and more recently as 'revived' and/or 'de-sequestered'. Consideration is given to an all-pervasive media culture, replete with images of death, and on-line social networks and technologies that offer the opportunity to inform, connect and re-connect society to death related issues. Equally, changes in societal institutions and cultural thinking, for instance in relation to science and religion, whose discourses have supported humanity in making sense of death for centuries are now being challenged and offer new opportunities for innovative thinking.

Similarly, literature that locates the position and value of children and childhood in Western society, is also presented. The combined might of developmental psychology and sociology, alongside socially embedded attitudes have variously placed the child as immature, dependent, becoming and innocent. Moving towards an opposition of these long established discourses and instead promoting competence, interdependence and participation is a central feature of this book and the research study within it. The new sociology of childhood, as mentioned earlier, advocates these virtues in conjunction with listening to children, thus providing opportunities to challenge traditional thinking and offer the emergence of new and contemporary viewpoints.

Attempts to connect youth and death have been made but the space afforded them is often rarefied; confined to either the child's cognitive understanding or the theorising of bereavement within the context of significant biographical events. However, more mainstream approaches are now being called for, which offer to incorporate a range of deaths from within the ordinary context of young-people's everyday lives, and these are clearly relevant here. Despite the assumed exclusivity of both death and childhood they can be identified as sharing similar features, those of marginalisation, sequestration and dichotomous thinking. This book, I hope, will bring both youth and death in from these margins and connect them through the power of conversation.

Having developed the above arguments, the chapter concludes by reflecting upon the framework and methods used in this study to open up a dialogue with these young-people. The metaphor of the stained glass window, emphasises how an eclectic mix of ideas can provide a sensitive methodological approach and a practical and caring foundation for research in this area. The inclusion of material artefacts as a method to encourage friendly and relaxed exchanges of ideas is discussed and despite leaving a discussion of ethics to the end of this chapter it is positioned as paramount throughout the study.

The following 3 chapters present the collected conversations. These, I suggest, are the highlight of and justification for this book and are more than worthy of the word-count given over to them. Chapter 3 focuses on various types of media and their influence on young-peoples' understanding of death and dying. Media deaths are highly visible sources of information in both real life representations and fictional portrayals. Such sources provide a multiplicity of stories, which utilise dominant societal discourses or 'cultural scripts' (Seale 1998: 2) on death. The prevalence of such scripts within media narratives were identified by young-people who were keen to adopt, adapt and confront them. Literature, film and news media gave them the opportunity to imagine, rehearse, try on and ultimately challenge dominant social constructions of death, through engagement with heroic, glamorous, violent and romanticised images and contrast them with their own lived reality. The media provide an 'omnipresent' (Hanusch 2010: 2) source of information about death for young-people, which can shape and reflect societal attitudes. However, young-people are not passive receivers of these representations but actively, creatively and positively construct their own perspectives on death.

Chapter 4 brings death 'up close and personal' as more intimate and private perspectives replace the explicitly public face of death discussed in the previous chapter. Young-people tell diverse stories, narrating their own personal encounters with death from close relatives to much-loved pets. Supported and encouraged by their friends a range of emotional responses are evident, as experiences are recounted and responded to with anger, sadness, silence and indeed a great deal of humour. Fears and claims of universally negative reactions, often used as a reason for not discussing death at all, are thereby challenged. New ways of relating to and thinking about death emerge from the sharing of experiences, and co-constructed ideas shed new light onto established ways of thinking. Furthermore, some of the more unusual material objects, provide unique, distinctive and rare glimpses into the death related thinking of these young-people. The final part of the chapter, perhaps surprisingly, concludes with young-people considering their own deaths. They candidly discuss how they might die, how they would like to be remembered, possibilities for their corpse and what rituals they think would best suit the lives they had led. Death, previously seen, and up to this point situated as 'other', becomes very much orientated to 'self'.

Personal reflections on scientific, religious and existential questions provide the focus for Chap. 5. Whilst Maddrell and Sidaway (2010) use the term 'deathscape' to illustrate the many sites, places and spaces of death, the meanings associated with them and the intersection between their private and often very public nature, I reimagine the term by appropriating it for similar internal landscapes of death. Such vistas are clearly illustrated in these conversations and are testament to a variety of changeable views, values and attitudes from both private and public discourses, which sometimes but not always, help to create a meaningful world in a life that ultimately leads to extinction. That death is inevitable and often feared is exposed as both a societal and a specifically personal issue. Furthermore, the avoidance of death as a topic of conversation between the generations is identified as a misplaced attempt by adults to 'lie' to children in order to protect them. Throughout these conversations, mortality can be, and is, understandably viewed in negative terms, however alternative positions, which see it as a unifying and meaningful part of human life, are also discussed. The final stages of Chap. 5, see the young-people tackle scientific and religious arguments, which often include or reject the possibilities of an afterlife. Such ideas are often situated in opposition to each other but here take-on a creative, co-constructed and negotiated form. Whilst some young-people firmly believe in an afterlife and others do not, the conversations highlight the possibility of both ideas existing side-by-side and therefore a flexibility of understanding that offers inclusive and eclectic ideas from both individual and group thinking.

The final chapter in this book offers some concluding reflections and further insights into the valuable and colourful contributions that these young-people have made to our understanding of their everyday encounters with death. It suggests that the study on which this text is based briefly offered a stage upon which the participants could participate in discussions of mortality on their own terms. Death was open for exploration in whatever direction the young-people wished to take it, and for a short time it was literally being encouraged out of the box, in order to encounter new voices on an age-old topic.

Just as Kastenbaum and Fox (2007) contend that adults assume children do not, cannot and should not think about death, this book hopes to illustrate the creative and expressive ways in which young-people can, do and perhaps should talk about death. The narratives represented challenge adult conjecture through the keen enthusiasm and willingness of these young-people to take part, the ways in which they engage with this topic, and the rich portrayals of the presence of death in their everyday lives. Silverman contends that we are 'deaf and mute to children's thoughts about death', and furthermore 'what a great disrespect this is, to ignore the child's reality' (2000: 3). Surely she is right.

References

Becker, E. (1973). *The denial of death*. New York: The Free Press.

Beit-Hallahmi, B. (2011). Ambivalent teaching and painful learning: Mastering the facts of life (?). In V. Talwar, P. Harris, & M. Schleifer (Eds.), *Children's understanding of death: From biological to religious conceptions*. New York: Cambridge University Press.

Berridge, K. (2002). *Vigor mortis*. London: Profile Books.

Bluebond-Langer, M. (1978). *The private worlds of dying children*. Princeton: Princeton University Press.

Cockburn, T. (2005). Children and the feminist ethic of care. *Childhood, 12*(1), 71–89.

Dickson-Swift, V., James, E. L., & Liamputtong, P. (2008). *Undertaking sensitive research in the health and social sciences: Managing boundaries, emotions and risk*. Cambridge: Cambridge University Press.

Douglas, M. ([1966] 2002). *Purity and danger*. Abingdon: Routledge.

Elias, N. (1985). *The loneliness of the dying*. New York: Continuum.

Faulkner, J. (2011). *The importance of being innocent: Why we worry about children*. Port Melbourne: Cambridge University Press.

Fearnley, R. (2012). *Communicating with children when a parent is at the end-of-life*. London: Jessica Kingsley.

Fisher, S. (2009). Motionless body. In S. Earle, C. Komaromy, & C. Bartholomew (Eds.), *Death and dying: A reader*. London: Sage.

Frank, A. W. (2010). *Letting stories breathe: A socio-narratology*. Chicago: The University of Chicago Press.

Gallacher, L., & Gallagher, M. (2008). Methodological immaturity in childhood research? Thinking through 'participatory methods'. *Childhood, 15*(4), 499–516.

Gorer, G. (1955). The pornography of death.*Encounter.*

Gorer, G. (1965). *Death, grief and mourning in contemporary britain.* London: Cresset.

Hanusch, F. (2010). *Representing death in the news: Journalism, media and mortality.* Basingstoke: Palgrave Macmillan.

Hockey, J. (2007). Closing in on Death? Reflections on research and researchers in the field of death and dying. *Health Sociology Review. 16*(5), 436–446.

Hockey, J., Komaromy, C., & Woodthorpe, K. (2010). Materialising absence. In J. Hockey, C. Komaromy, & K. Woodthorpe (Eds.), *The matter of death: Space, place and materiality.* Basingstoke: Palgrave MacMillan.

Hunter, S., & Smith, D. (2008). Predictors of children's understandings of death: Age, cognitive ability, death experience and maternal communicative competence. *Omega—Journal of Death and Dying, 57*(2), 143–162.

Kastenbaum, R., & Fox, L. (2007). Do imaginary companions die? An exploratory study. *Omega—Journal of Death and Dying, 56* (2), 123–152.

Kellahear, A. (2007). The end of death in late modernity: An emerging public health challenge. *Critical Public Health, 17*(1), 71–79.

Kellehear, A. (Ed.). (2009). *The study of dying: From autonomy to transformation.* Cambridge: Cambridge University Press.

Kemp, A. R. (2014). *Death, dying and bereavement in a changing world.* New Jersey, US: Pearson.

Lee, R. (2008). Modernity, Mortality and re-enchantment: The death taboo revisited. *Sociology, 42*(4), 745–759.

Lee, R. M. (1993). *Doing research on sensitive topics.* London: Sage.

Maddrell, A., & Sidaway, J. D. (2010). *Deathscapes: Spaces for death, dying, mourning and remembrance.* Surrey: Ashgate.

McManus, R. (2013). *Death in a global age.* Basingstoke: Palgrave Macmillan.

Mellor, P. A., & Shilling, C. (1993). Modernity, self-identity and the sequestration of death. *Sociology, 27*(3), 411–431.

Plummer, K. (2001). *Documents of life 2: An invitation to critical humanism.* London: Sage.

Ribbens McCarthy, J. (2006). *Young-people's experiences of loss and bereavement: Towards an interdisciplinary approach.* Berkshire: Open University Press.

Seale, C. (1998). *Constructing death: The sociology of dying and bereavement.* Cambridge: Cambridge University Press.

Silverman, P. R. (2000). *Never too young to know.* Oxford: Oxford University Press.

Tronto, J. C. ([1993] 2009). *Moral boundaries: A political argument for an ethic of care*. London: Routledge.

United Nations Convention on the Rights of the Child. (1989). Retrieved January 2, 2013, from http://www.un.org/documents/ga/res/44/a44r025. htm.

Uprichard, E. (2010). Questioning research with children: Discrepancy between theory and practice? *Children and Society, 24,* 3–13.

Wall, J. (2010). *Ethics: In the light of childhood*. Washington, DC: Georgetown University Press.

Walter, T. (1994). *The revival of death*. London: Routledge.

Woodthorpe, K. (2008). Sociological Eye On … The Sexiness of Topics: What it means to be 'into' death. *Network Newsletter of the British Sociological Association,* Autumn. Retrieved April 23, 2013, from http://www.britsoc. co.uk/media/27022/Sociological_Eye_on_Death.pdf.

2

Improper or Proper Conversations?

Introduction

The cultural positioning of death as an improper topic of conversation, in particular for the young, has numerous consequences, not least being a lack of opportunity to examine how such conversations might be realised. The purpose of this chapter is therefore to explore why death has been, and often still is, constructed in this way, and equally to examine how discussions on this topic might be achieved with young-people. The first goal is met by examining a variety of literature, which offers to shed light onto the many and often paradoxical discourses surrounding both death and childhood in modern Western societies. It is perhaps only by taking this intriguing literary journey that it is possible to consider these two seemingly disparate entities as potentially similar, particularly in the ways they have been problematised, marginalised, romanticised and sequestered by society and academia alike. The obvious and often poignantly stark relationship between death and youth has understandably led to conversations in this area being particularly focused on individual experiences of significant loss, bereavement, grief and illness with no hope of cure. These are of course essential,

© The Author(s) 2017
S. Coombs, *Young People's Perspectives on End-of-Life*,
Studies in Childhood and Youth, DOI 10.1007/978-3-319-53631-6_2

fundamental, and ethical discussions but here I ask a more mundane question, that is, what do we know of the more ordinary, everyday and commonplace ways in which death makes its entrances and exits into and out of the lives of young-people, and equally how do we find out? This is the initial focus of the chapter before moving on to explore the theoretical, methodological and ethical considerations embedded in my attempt to uncover young-peoples' perspectives on the end-of-life and make an improper topic of conversation, proper, which I refer to here as my journey through the stained glass window.

First, the literature and the purposeful inclusion of myriad view-points, exposing the reader to a labyrinth of changing ideas from across these two spheres of knowledge, death and childhood. Initially drawn from the highly influential work of social historian Phillipe Ariès (1974, 1981/2008) this chapter examines key debates in the sociology of death, alongside changing societal attitudes. Well-established discourses, which frame the emergence of death as denied and positioned as the taboo topic of twentieth century are challenged as evidence is uncovered for the ubiquitous presence of death in society and in particular its lavish representation in the media. These contrasting views situate the chapter in complex and contested spaces, which position death, arguably the most static of concepts, as one of the most dynamic.

In addition to death's vibrant field of enquiry a number of prominent motifs and theoretical conceptualisations of children and childhood are examined. Ariès (1962) is called upon yet again, this time to illustrate the historical emergence of childhood as a stage different to and separate from adulthood. Consideration is given to traditional views from the disciplines of developmental psychology and sociology, which position childhood within the confines of difference, incompetence and inade-quacy. In defiance of such entrenched theorising, the emergence of the 'new paradigm in the sociology of childhood' (James and Prout 1997) cast doubt on how childhood had been explored, addressed and concep-tualised, and instead featured and promoted children's voices, rights and participation.

The literary journey draws to a close by examining texts that bring death and childhood together. Research and practice in this area has moved on apace, yet remains less common than encounters with adult experience, and this is particularly so within the context of listening directly to children, unless they have been bereaved or are living with a life-limiting condition. Over the centuries the close relationship between children and death has been witnessed and acknowledged in all its horror, but changing patterns of mortality and societal attitudes towards both death and childhood have meant a reduction in children's involvement with personal deaths and a subsequent reluctance from adults to discuss death and dying with them.

Listening to disparate voices from across the sociologies of death and childhood, and where the boundaries allow an integration of the two, brings together complex, subtle and fascinating viewpoints. Death is clearly not an inert concept, although in reality it may take on this quality, and childhood remains an equally erratic notion, despite adult desires to pin it down. The uncertain and changing nature of both, leads to complexities for adults, who often look back nostalgically on their childhood but with uncertainty towards death. This leaves adults vulnerable, as the ambiguity of their relationship with both the start-of-life in the form of childhood and the end-of-life, leads to an uncertainty concerning the propriety of death as topic of conversation with the young. Young-people also populate this liminal insecurity, surrounded everyday by multiple forms of death but equally aware that adults are trying to protect them from it. The final sections of this chapter explore how these uncertainties, presented throughout the literature, are met and negotiated in this research project. It positions the eclecticism of the stained glass window as providing a gateway into the deathscapes of young-people, and thereby challenges the notion of death as an improper topic of conversation with children.

Improper Conversations?

Positioning Death

Death has been and often still is, positioned as problematic for individuals, societies and academics alike. Gorer (1955, 1965) was among the first to examine societal attitudes towards death. He was influential in asserting that modern societies avoid and therefore deny death, and in so doing death had become a taboo topic. The effect of the taboo, he argued, was to push death to the margins of society, only for it to re-emerge in illicit forms that rendered it pornographic, thereby replacing sex as the foremost contemporary taboo of Western society. Following on from Gorer's work further problems arise. Berger and Luckmann propose that death 'posits the most terrifying threat to the taken-for-granted realities of everyday life' (1967/1991: 119). Becker that the fear of death is universal, it 'haunts the human animal like nothing else' (1973: xvii). Howarth that 'death raises the problem of meaning for human beings' (2007: 15) and Yalom, that 'mortality has haunted us from the beginning of history' (2008: 1). Death is situated in a context of fear, denial, sequestration and notions of taboo. However, these ideas are not without their critics, as we shall see. In the meantime, I draw upon the work of the influential social historian Phillipe Ariès to examine how some of these changes came about.

Ariès' Interpretation

The continually altering landscape of human experience and understanding in relation to mortality is vividly captured by Philippe Ariès in his historical accounts of *Western Attitudes towards Death: From the Middle Ages to the Present* (1974) and *The Hour of Our Death* (1981/2008). Over the last thousand years, he argues that, the human relationship with death has constantly evolved and changed and fluctuations in religious beliefs, societal structures, philosophical and scientific thought, art and literature have all played their part. His categorisation of four Western death cultures into different epochs: the 'tame death', 'death of the self', 'death of the other', and 'invisible death' or 'death denied', is useful in setting the scene for the evolution of the phenomenon of death denial that he outlines, and helps to trace the development of death from familiar collective destiny to a hidden and shameful secret.

Religion was, and arguably still is, central to any discussion on conceptualising death and makes up a significant part of Ariès' argument. The history of death in Europe is inevitably concerned with the

Christian treatment of it, with little or no account being taken of other parts of the world and their religions, thus restricting wider understanding. Religion, Ariès contends, was the hub of life and death in the Middle Ages, the church taking the lead in officiating at human entrances and exits. Complex funeral rituals expressed the continuing relationship of the living with the dead, the church on earth and the church in heaven. Similarly, in an effort to find room to bury more bodies around sacred sites, the living and the dead literally rubbed shoulders, as the bodies of the previously deceased were exhumed and their bones put on display in galleries that became popular meeting places. Death in the early middle ages was therefore highly visible, familiar and public. Ariès evokes a 'household sort of death' (1974: 14) in which the spectacle of death and the personal implications of it made little impression on the living.

Ariès characterises death within this era as 'tamed'. He explains that a passive acceptance of collective destiny was central to this time and the expectation of death involved little more than an extended sleep followed by an assured resurrection on the final Day of Judgment. As the Christian tradition situates death and resurrection as delivery from evil, death was/is given meaning in this way, and without this justification it becomes a 'savage force' (Staudt 2009a: 6) from which 'denial' emerges in defence.

The period of time extending from the thirteenth to the fifteenth century, Ariès terms 'la mort de soi', the death of the self, an epoch in which individuality took precedence over collectivism. Death now tainted the enjoyment of life, it ceased to be a form of repose and instead became associated with physical suffering, decomposition and painful separation. In Ariès' words, attitudes moved from death as 'an awareness and summation of life, to death as an awareness and desperate love of this life' (1981/2008: 138–139).

The following era, 'la mort de toi', thy death or the death of others, emerged gradually in the fifteenth and continued into the nineteenth century. This period illustrates how tamed, familiar, tangible, everyday death gave way to an admirable, beautiful, passionate and even erotic event, which warranted emotional expressions of love and grief. A 'sentimental landslide' that took the focus of death away from the individual to those around them and started a romantic era of death that found the twin concepts of Eros and Thanatos, love and death, inextricably bound together. Death, Ariès comments, is 'transformed into the highest beauty' (1981/2008: 611), and long held beliefs connecting sin, evil, death, punishment and hell begin to break down. Death becomes a place of re-union and matters of belief or non-belief are immaterial. Christian paradise, psychic phenomena, spirituality or memories, Ariès asserts, 'They have all built the same castle, in the image of earthly homes' (1981/2008: 611) places where they will be re-united with those they love.

Ariès' final epoch describes a 'brutal revolution', an 'unheard-of phenomenon' (1974: 85), whereby from the mid-nineteenth century onward the familiar face of death disappears under a carpet of lies. He contends that Western society seeks to hide the ugliness and unbearable emotion of death. Life must be seen as happy; there is no room for death, or the dying person. He argues that 'the process of hushing-up had begun' (1974: 87). Death is now unnameable, forbidden, and the remit of professionals, who take on the role of 'the masters of death' (1974: 89). The emotional site of death is private and secret, and moreover it becomes essential that society does not notice that death has occurred. The environment of sorrow is a sign of mental instability and significantly, even within the family, must be avoided 'for fear of upsetting the children' (1974: 90). Death in all its guises, he argues, had become taboo.

Ariès clearly plays a significant role in the analysis of death and his contribution to the rise of the death-denial thesis is clear. His evaluation of changing ideas brings the reader to last quarter of the twentieth century where he paints an increasingly bleak picture, in which death has become hidden in institutions and governed by medical professionals. The great dramatic 'end scene', so evident for many hundreds of years, he argues, is now protracted, dissected and devoid of meaning, and the moment and the circumstance of death is sanitised to avoid any emotional or embarrassing scenes that should not be conducted in public. Funeral rites have been modified and made discreet, mourning is reduced to a secret, solitary and lonely space and outward sorrow inspires only pity and repugnance. Ariès argues that these more recent phenomena are impositions, which prohibit what was once required and impose a state of happiness in order to suppress death.

Ariès' detailed account provides a historical appreciation of the changing nature of Western societal relationships with death. He outlines the journey of dominant discourses from acceptance, inspired by traditional Christian religious beliefs and supported by the church, to fear, denial and sequestration, due he argues, to the loss of these very same traditions. In response, he contends that humanity's subsequent search for meaning results in an emphasis on medical science to prolong life, and therefore conceal its failures from public view, that is those who are dying, and ultimately death. McManus (2013) contends that evaluating historical accounts, such as this, are useful in depicting how death changes over time, what influences such changes, and how these changes inform death in the present. The positioning of an 'improper conversation'.

Death Denied?

The fear of death and the presence of the highly influential death denial thesis are well established in modern Western society. I have indicated how both the historical works of Ariès, and the anthropological work of Gorer are central to describing its rise. However, psychological accounts derived from the work of Freud in the 1940s have been and remain significant in their contribution to explaining Western approaches to death, and in particular to the idea of death denial. Becker's (1973) psychoanalytic lens focused on the capacity of humans to think symbolically outside and beyond themselves, whilst simultaneously recognising the finite nature of their lives. He argues that the fear and terror experienced by such thoughts leads to death denial acting as a defence mechanism against such existential anxiety. McManus (2013) suggests that a more 'macro-orientated' view of death-denial can be found in the work of Mellor and Shilling (1993), in which modern Western death is characterised and organised through professionalisation, medicalisation and individuation. This latter approach emphasises a different aspect of death denial, situating it as hidden rather than forbidden but equally improper.

Therefore, situated in and alongside the proposition of continued death denial is the sequestration thesis, a key concern in the field of death studies, and one that has generated substantial literature and debate amongst sociologists within contemporary Western societies (Giddens 1991; Mellor 1993; Mellor and Shilling 1993). This argument contends that 'death has been removed from the public sphere and located instead in the private world of the individual' (Howarth 2007: 24). In his consideration of 'fateful moments' (1991: 202) such as birth and death, Giddens argues that death tends to be the more hidden of the two as it threatens our everyday understanding of ourselves as humans with a place in the world, our ontological security; Mellor and Shilling observe that 'death passes virtually unnoticed most of time' (1993: 417). Therefore, in response to the challenges that death places before us, or as McManus contends, the 'chaos that lurks behind our need to make our own meaning' (2013: 25), the threat of death is hidden away. In the face of the sheer incomprehension of death, Valentine argues that 'we are thrown back on our own individual resources rather than the community to cope with the threat death poses to our sense of ontological security' (2006: 70).

Mellor and Shilling's (1993) argument links a rising identification of the self and the body, plus an upsurge in secularisation, with a tendency to privatise experiences of death. In accordance with this proposition, and in similar ways to Ariès, Gorer and Becker, Mellor and Shilling argue that the decline of the sacred has left individuals struggling to establish meanings and values in their everyday lives and as a consequence has led to a focus on self-identity via the continual construction and re-construction of self-narratives as a way to establish a consistency and meaning in life. Central to this has been the greater sense of value put on the body in contrast to religious frameworks, which constructed existential and ontological certainties outside of it. With religion arguably in decline in Western societies, the body has become a bearer or symbolic value and a constituent part of the self, in which youthful, sexual and beautiful bodies are prized above others. The presence of death clearly becomes highly problematic within this framework, undermining our taken-for-granted day-to-day reality.

Throughout their argument Mellor and Shilling continue to highlight the 'strengthening of boundaries between living and dying bodies, and a diminution of the sacred in modern societies' (1993: 424) as factors that provide a tendency towards sequestration. Alongside of these, they draw upon Bauman's 'policies of survival' (1992: 13), which include a modern reluctance to come into contact with the dying, the medicalisation of death, a cultural orientation to youth and the reluctance of parents to discuss death with their children. Such strategies, they contend, are attempts to keep death at bay by denying it through a variety of options orientated around the health and survival of the body, leaving no time for individuals to contemplate death itself. This all-pervasive anxiety around health, life and delaying death leads to death being understood through highly privatised and individual medical causes such as cancer, heart disease and high blood pressure, thus negating the possibility of death through natural mortality, which arguably represents the further sequestration of death itself. Likewise, the variety of individual deaths witnessed within the media only serves to further fragment the meaning of death (Walter 1991), and as Mellor and Shilling contend, such individual causes, cases and circumstances 'encourage the view of death as avoidable and contingent' (1993: 425), and therefore are reassuring rather than threatening. However, as they go on to argue, in conditions of high modernity where biographical narratives are continually reflexive the fragility of survival narratives and their ultimate futility are apparent. Therefore, the threat of death returns and humans are left struggling to face mortality alone. Consequently, death has become, if not wholeheartedly taboo, then secluded and sequestered, in order for people to go about their everyday business unhindered by continual existential uncertainty.

However, the sequestration thesis is not without its critics. Walter (1994) disagrees with Mellor and Shilling's argument that the individualisation of death has led to it being hidden, sequestered and therefore ultimately denied. For him the individualisation of death means, as his book title of the same year indicates, *The Revival of Death*, rather than an attempt to hide it. Walter contends that death is everywhere, particularly in the mass media, but also in 'the authority of the individual ...only individuals can determine how they want to die or grieve'

(1994: 185). Therefore, even more recently he argues that there is room to resist Mellor and Shilling's argument, that 'death, like madness and other fateful moments, has been sequestered, put in a box, to protect society' (Walter 2008a: 324).

Similarly, Stanley and Wise claim that, the sequestration thesis has become a 'juggernaut' that has taken on 'canonical qualities', frequently being highlighted as 'facts (rather than arguments)' (2011: 948). In their attempt to re-theorise the sequestration thesis they draw upon the work of Elias, *The Loneliness of Dying* (1985) and *The Civilising Process* (1939/2000). With this foundation, they contend that despite sequestration occurring through aspects of death being gradually drawn away from the domestic sphere and into institutional contexts, the ubiquity of these have not totally replaced the importance of the domestic space.

They argue that Elias's approach to the theorisation of death provides a different way of seeing sequestration that emphasises how social change, throughout modernity, has had an impact on how death is viewed and meanings constructed. These changes, they contend, include life being viewed as an organised and predictable event and death as the inevitable but nevertheless 'final stage of [this] long orderly process' (Stanley and Wise 2011: 951). More unusual or extreme types of death, often associated with violence, pain and unpredictability, are experienced by others, not us. Equally, even though a high degree of proposed individualised meaning making is evident within society, Elias suggests that this masks the dependence of people on each other and the interdependencies that bind them together. Stanley and Wise extend this by suggesting that people respond to death and dying within the context of 'networks' and 'interpersonal relationships' (2011: 948), which centre on and extend from the domestic sphere. Building on Elias's paradigm, they are able to argue that individualisation and interdependency are intertwined. Death and absence, therefore form part of the 'complex interminglings' (2011: 948) of both private and public aspects of dying, bereavement and mourning, and constitute a network of relationships concerned with the familiar and every day, bringing 'out there' and 'in here' together (2011: 953).

The sequestration debate will undoubtedly continue, but the combined analysis of Stanley, Wise and Elias acknowledges a number of important factors. Namely, people respond to death and dying within networks of others and personal relationships and not purely as individuals. Sequestration, whilst a powerful force within civil-institutional contexts, continues alongside death's place in the domestic space, and the widespread fascination, if not obsession, with death in the media. In this space the bonds of relationships continue within the contexts in which they were lived out, and everyday ontological understandings in relation to death and dying are constructed. Stanley and Wise therefore contend that the process of sequestration is complex and contradictory, and notwithstanding the influence of civil-institutional organisations, the continued presence and activities carried out within the domestic sphere and networks of families and friends reach out to merge and mingle with both private and public components of death in contemporary Western society.

However, claims as to the death denying nature of contemporary Western societies continue. Kellahear (2007) argues that the 'cosmopolitan age' continues to deny, or turn its back on those who die in nursing homes, those stigmatised by HIV/AIDS, and those dying from old age with disabling and chronic diseases. Conversely, Walter argues that, 'personal expression' (1991: 297) in relation to death is returning, and that stories of death are being encouraged, told and listened to (1994). Howarth (2007) argues that the ubiquitous public presence of death, via, cinema, television, literature, documentaries and news media challenges the death-denial thesis, and raises important questions in relation to the supposedly hidden nature of death. She observes that, death is 'complex and multifaceted', that is appears in both public and private spheres in forms 'expected and unexpected', 'natural and unnatural', 'complex and simple' and therefore cannot be reduced to 'a single, simple discourse' (2007: 35). More recently, Staudt argues that 'the pendulum between concealment and recognition has swung in favour of recognition' (2009a: 4), and it is to this I now turn.

Death Recognised

Forty year on from Ariès' initial claims it is possible to contend that change is now afoot in both academic thinking and societal responses to death. It is clear that challenges have, and continue to be made, in relation to the supposed taboo nature of death, the notion of universal fear, and the extent to which sequestration occurs in contemporary society. It is equally clear that death, dying and mourning do not have static meanings and are continuously changing and developing. Although popular discourses continue to suggest that, in some cases, death is alternately taboo, denied and sequestered, commentators such as Walter (1991) argue that social scientists are having second thoughts. He contends that the death taboo is 'grossly overdrawn and lacking in subtlety' (1991: 297) and indeed somewhat strange when considering the plethora of end-of-life headlines encountered across the daily papers. He suggests it is a mistake to state universally that 'modern society cannot cope with death' and instead argues that 'it deals with it very nicely thank you, with its elevation of youth, education and progress' (1991: 306). However, he does go on to argue that the increasing social acceptance of death is accompanied by an intense individual pain that few are willing to share.

Noys (2005) also denounces the idea that death is a hidden feature of modernity. He reveals contemporary exposure to death using a variety of examples: the rise in popularity of crime fiction, media images of bodies jumping from the World Trade Centre during 9/11, the controversy around the public autopsy performed by Professor Gunther Von Hagens on November 20, 2002, and fascination with the Holocaust, zombies and confrontational avant-garde art. Noys, in a similar way to Gorer before him, argues that the more we try to push death away, the more it invades our culture, in 'traumatic forms' (2005: 25). Equally, Kellehear testifies that we cannot hide from witnessing a rise in 'shameful' (2007: 8) forms of dying, those stigmatised by poverty, ageing and social exclusion, and negatively labelled by others. He argues that whilst prosperous Westerners, who live longer, medically managed lives are able to shield themselves from death to some extent, nonetheless diseases such as HIV/AIDS ravage developing countries, and the rising tide of dementia remains a constant threat and cause of concern to the affluent.

In accordance with Walter (2008b), I argue that the dead are more present in society now than before, and in support of Noys that the 'prudery' (2005: 2) associated with death is being, however slowly, replaced by new and exciting ways of approaching this complex topic. However, Noys indicates caution, highlighting the problematic nature of simplistic either/or accounts, and arguing that death is both 'invisible' and 'highly visible' in a multiplicity of intricate, yet everyday ways, in modern Western culture. That humans have always been exposed to death is clear, but contemporary exposure to death is manifested in a number of new and emerging ways, which I now explore.

Berridge argues that death is, 'moving from the margins of society to the mainstream', is 'becoming social not anti-social, public not private, fashionable not fearful, death is the focus of a new permissiveness. Death is in' (2002: 26). Howarth (2007) also comments on the renewed popularity and recognition of mortality in Western societies. She points to a lively entertainment industry and a vibrant news media for bringing a variety of new ways of death into our lives. Similarly, Lee (2008) taking a wider remit, refers to a flourishing research culture into human mortality, an increase in academic programmes related to the topic, a lively interest in near-death experiences, the spread of the hospice movement and the subsequent awareness of end-of-life care, plus a deluge of cinematic interpretations. Death, Walter (2008b) argues, has a very public presence in modern society, and Staudt contends that 'we can justifiably say that the twenty-first century is well on its way to giving birth to yet a new episteme of death' (2009a: 13).

A central feature of our renewed exposure to death lies, Staudt argues, in its 'visual ubiquity' (2009a: 15) via new technologies, which bring death directly into our homes in numbers not previously imagined. Similarly, Walter highlights the prominence of death in the media, suggesting that 'death, disaster, murder and mourning are staple diets of both upmarket and downmarket mass media' (2009: 3.1). An abundance of books and academic articles attest to the central role death plays in popular culture. For example, death in the news media (Hanusch 2008, 2010), cinematic versions of dying (Knox 2006; McInerney 2009), death in art (Gittings 2009), celebrity deaths (Foltyn 2008; Walter 2009; Davies 2010), and the ubiquitous nature of death in television soaps, shows and documentaries (Howarth 2007). In this way, Howarth (2007) argues, the media both support and challenge the traditional and dominant frameworks of death, such as science and religion, whilst promoting new and alternative approaches to death. And yet, despite an increased attentiveness to death, and the media's ready projection of it, Staudt suggests that our 'awakening and awareness are not synonymous with personal acceptance and acculturation' (2009b: 180).

The rise of the internet within advanced industrial societies has also provided an emergent space for death to display its wares and highlight its presence. The internet has become a source for both information in relation to death and dying and a repository for mourning. Death is not only a physical event but also very much a social one, resulting in the disruption of social networks, and a restructuring of social engagement for the bereaved (Walter et al. 2011). The term 'social network' now more frequently alludes to virtual, as opposed to actual spaces, and nowadays the internet has become an increasingly social space. Howarth (2007) suggests that these real and newly emerging virtual spaces act to assist communities in learning about and raising awareness of diverse approaches and responses to death. Walter et al. reflect that the users of such sites may value them as a form of 'sanctuary' (2011: 278), away from professionals and/or family. Online memorial sites have increased in popularity, but are now far outnumbered by more general social networking sites such as Facebook. Walter et al. also argue that via new technologies such as computer screens, iPads and mobile phones, all connected to the World Wide Web, the dead become part of our everyday online world, unlike those seen on TV who are rarely known to us. The dead we typically encounter on Facebook are those personally known to our particular online networks, this allows for expressions of grief and communication with others in a public rather than private forum. The phenomenal rise of interactive social media has seen, Walter et al. argue, the re-emergence of initially public and increasingly communal grief. Interestingly, Howarth (2007) points out that these emergent communities often utilise, adopt and adapt traditional rituals of remembrance. The placing of flowers, the lighting of candles or the leaving of ephemera in the form of messages, all of which are available in real or virtual memorial spaces, supports this point. Walter et al. conclude that twenty-first century media have the capacity to 'desequester' the dying, death and mourning, by bringing death back into everyday life but equally suggest caution in acclaiming each new technology as 'humankind's new saviour' (2011: 291).

Although the media and information technology have been central in their promotion of other and sometimes unusual accounts of death, levels of religiosity and spirituality clearly remain a matter of importance within the realms of contemporary death and dying. As we have seen, literature attests to the proposal that modernity has developed alongside desacralisation and yet, it has failed to replace religious beliefs with the scientific certainties of objective truth, knowledge and proof, which is clearly problematic for the great unknown. Howarth (2007) situates the declining power of the established church, frequent challenges to the omnipotence of science and the firmly controlled boundaries between life and death as key drivers for the emergence of alternative spiritualties. Such 'new age' approaches, which have risen like a phoenix from the ashes, offer a greater diversity of connections to an afterlife, the possibility of continuing relationships between the living and the dead, an overall blurring of the boundaries between life and death, and a challenge that offers new and alternatives approaches to contemporary death and dying.

In concluding this section, it has become clear that the last decade of the twentieth century and the first decade of the twenty-first have seen huge changes in the way death and dying have been treated and represented in everyday and academic spheres. Our ability to 'chat death stuff' is clearly dependent on contextual influences. Fear of death is readily claimed as universal and death as taboo, resulting in denial and sequestration. Yet, as noted, alternative views are pitched in opposition and construct death as part of collective, interconnected and newly emerging deathways. On the one hand, the individual, now in communion with others has become the expert, rather than the previously dominant institutions of science and religion, which it has been argued, have worked together to marginalise experiences of death and dying. On the other hand, the media have brought about collectivities, connections and networks where death is emerging in a 'rich fusion of beliefs, practices and rituals that is resurrecting death and beginning to embrace mortality as central to life' (Howarth 2007: 266). Claims that death is individualised and sequestered hardly seem an appropriate claim in a world of intense media coverage, real and virtual networks of people, and the promotion of continuing relationships with the dead. Surely then death is an appropriate topic of conversation for anyone… but is it?

Positioning Childhood

Following on from the intrigue of end-of-life discussions this section moves on to consider key debates surrounding children and childhood. This is something we might profess to know more about, as unlike death, we have been there. As J. M. Barrie, in his famous work *Peter Pan and Wendy* pronounces, these are 'magic shores', on which 'we can still hear the sound of the surf, though we shall land no more'(1911/1988: 5). Exploring these once again complex, overlapping and intertwining perspectives highlights the attitudes and relationships of adults with children and vice versa. Therefore, in a similar way to death and dying, children and childhood are seen through a number of different lenses, and a variety of epistemes created.

Primarily, children have been, and continue to be viewed as 'other' than adults, and childhood as different, needing to be constrained and contained via 'physical, conceptual and moral boundaries' (James et al. 1998: 38). Jenks insists that the child is 'familiar to us and yet strange' (1996: 3), and similarly, writing in 2005, that children are viewed as out of the ordinary, different and special, and as a consequence are marginalised in society and in mainstream sociology. Children themselves are often of little interest to anyone, other than as future adults, and childhood is constructed and reconstructed in ways that highlight specific differences from the 'grown-up' world. Today however, the situation is changing, and journals, academic courses and a multiplicity of textbooks bear witness to the increased interest in children and childhood, both as an academic subject and in everyday life. More recently, A. L. James maintains that 'although children are set aside from adults, they are not, should not and cannot be set apart from adults' (2010: 494). Changing views of childhood have, in earlier periods, been well documented, for example in the work of Ariès, who once again will be used as a starting point, this time in discovering how attitudes towards childhood have changed over time. Walter comments that Ariès 'single-handedly first created one historical specialism (childhood), then popularised another (death)—an unparalleled achievement' (1991: 297). His primacy in both these spheres indicates the importance of his work here and situates it at the forefront of these discussions.

Ariès' Interpretation

Over 50 years ago, although arguably little has changed, Ariès notes that the contemporary world is 'obsessed by the physical, moral and sexual problems of childhood' (1962: 411), whilst at the same time declaring that this was not always the case. Through his interpretations of medieval art, in which depictions of children were scarce, he claimed that childhood did not exist as a separate category during this time. However, beginning in the thirteenth century, he notes a gradual change in representations, particularly drawings of the putto. This revival of the Hellenistic Eros, in the form of small, naked children, often with wings, became and remained extremely popular throughout the Renaissance and Baroque eras and is famously represented in the work of Raphael's Sistine Madonna (1513–1514). For Ariès, the importance of these little figures represents 'something far deeper than the taste for classical nudity, something that can be ascribed only to a broad surge of interest in childhood' (1962: 44). This early attention, Ariès contends, is followed in the sixteenth century by a phase in which the child is idolised and valued as a source of amusement and relaxation, especially for women. Subsequently, Ariès points to a period of moralism (16–18th century), the interest in childhood shifts yet again, from one of entertainment to one of 'psychological interest and moral solicitude' (1962: 131). Discipline and preparation for adulthood are now the order of the day, the child a weak and fragile creature, needs to be both safeguarded and reformed, not only in the present but also for the future, and the family and education are to play a central role in this.

Ariès argues, that during the sixteenth and seventeenth centuries, changing attitudes towards education and the family, positioned children as 'not ready for life'. The child was seen to need 'special treatment, a sort of quarantine, before he was allowed to join the adults', and equally, parents were taught that they were 'responsible before God for the souls, and indeed the bodies too, of their children' (1962: 412). This combination of the child's primacy within the family and formal education removed the child from adult society, and as a result childhood became marginalised.

Cosaro (2011), points-out the importance of Ariès' historical account, in creating both an interest in childhood that had long been neglected, and promoting a view of childhood as a social construction. Whilst Ariès' studies of childhood and indeed death are not without criticism, the changes and challenges he alludes to, help to uncover fluctuating societal views, behaviours and values, and thereby render both concepts dynamic. I suggest therefore, that these ideas are valuable and offer insights into the vacillating alienation between death and childhood, an appreciation of arguments concerning the propriety/impropriety of death as a topic of conversation for the young, and an understanding of the positions death and childhood occupy on the margins of society. Let us pursue this marginalised child further.

Childhood: Images and Perspectives

In accordance with such marginalization, Holt (1975) situates the institution of childhood within a safe and protected 'walled garden'. Faulkner (2011) portrays the garden as more perfect than God's Eden, with no snakes and no fruit, a place in which powerful adults can regulate the knowledge that separates innocence from worldliness. Similarly, Taylor calls to mind a utopian 'Neverland' to evoke 'that idealized and timeless childhood place of perfect harmony' (2011: 420). Holt denounces such perfect, protected and innocent childhoods as unrealistic and suggests placing gates in the garden walls in order to allow young-people, who find life inside it 'confining and humiliating', an opportunity to explore the world beyond.

Taylor (2011) concurs that the continuation of such nostalgic and romantic notions of childhood perpetuate the perception of the permanently good and innocent child and promote a protection-ist stance. James et al. suggest that the legacy of such thinking endows adults with the responsibility to uphold their children in a state of 'pris-tine innocence' (1998: 14), far removed from the hostility of the world around them. Thus, the immensely powerful vision of the Apollonian and unworldly child is maintained, described by Jenks as 'the heir to the sunshine and light, the espouser of poetry and beauty', a young per-son whose qualities are 'angelic, innocent and untainted by the world' (1996: 73). In response, Faulkner contends that adults promote and value this state of 'carefully crafted ignorance' (2011: 78–79) creating for their children an enchanted world, an undisturbed paradise.

Yet, society equally constructs another role for the child, one that is very different from the naivety described so far. Jenks (1996) refers to the Dionysian child, a child that is inherently knowing, evil and cor-rupt. Derived from Augustinian doctrine and the birth of original sin, this view is of a child prone to wickedness and transgression, a knowing child that needs firm control from the adults around them. Similarly, Freud's model of the human psyche, the composition of the self, via the id, ego and super-ego, constructs the realm of the id as a source of unconscious desires both sexual and aggressive, desires that demand satisfaction and instant gratification. Jenks contends that these three components of the self are formulated in such a way as to represent col-lectivity (the super-ego), the adult (the ego), and the child (id). Of the three the id, the child, is a 'dark driving force' that must be repressed (Jenks 1996: 72). Gittins (1998) argues that the continual denial of evil, darkness and violence within children, means that we fail to embrace 'growth' and 'wholeness', which constitute the child as both dark and light, good and evil, innocent and corrupt. However, Faulkner (2011) contends that when adults envisage children as 'polluted' in this way, they become 'disenchanted' with them; the child is seen as no longer belonging to the world of innocence and simplicity, their innocence is corrupted by knowledge. Knowledge and power are the remit of adults, and 'share with God the sovereign power to banish and send into exile the despoiled innocents we create' (Faulkner 2011: 79).

It is clear therefore that the concept of childhood itself, emerges from a variety of constructions and a number of perspectives, the results of which are illuminating. Perhaps the most prevalent of these approaches has been, and still is, developmental psychology and its attempt to understand children's behaviour scientifically. Under its auspices, children's cognitive, emotional and social lives are explored, measured and observed. Easily the most influential figure within this paradigm is that of Jean Piaget (1896–1980). Piaget's stages of cognitive development, formulated in the 1920s, offer an account that details a precise trajectory from concrete to abstract reasoning. Burman (2008) contends that no nurse, teacher, social worker or counsellor will have completed his or her training without learning about this highly influential theory. Notwithstanding the authority of Piaget's research, more recently less emphasis has been placed upon it, due in part to an 'industry of Piaget critique' (Burman 2008: 247). For example, James et al. argue that Piaget's theories produced the most 'materially reductive' (1998: 17) image of childhood that we are likely to encounter. The framework situates the child as irrational, illogical, incompetent and inadequate and quite obviously different from the real human beings, that is those who have 'grown-up' (James et al. 19938: 18). Furthermore, Jenks envisions the child as 'abandoned to theory', 'scientific rationality' and 'the tyrannical realm of fact' (1996: 25), at the expense of difference and social context.

From this perspective, it is clear that the ultimate task for the child is to develop, mature and 'become' an adult through naturally occurring biological changes. Close parallels, found within sociology suggest the child learns to conform to social norms through adult and institutional regulation, referred to as socialisation. James et al. define this process as 'the successful transmission of cultures from one generation to another' (1998: 23). Models of socialisation have a tendency towards determinism, often constructing the child as passive and relatively powerless. Significant others, such as parents, must impose the adult world on them (Wyness 2006). Even though socialisation theory may not offer the precision of developmental psychology in describing the process of growing-up, Wyness contends that it contains the same presumptions of the child as 'person-in-waiting' (2006: 140) rather than a person in their own right. Corsaro concurs that traditional socialisation relegates children to 'primarily passive roles' (2011: 29), which delay their entry into the adult world and situate them on the periphery of society.

The future orientation of childhood, which situates the young within a division of adult 'human beings' and child 'human becomings' (Lee 2001: 8), is much debated. Uprichard examines these, describing the 'becoming' child as 'explicitly future orientated', 'a future adult' rather than a 'young human being' (2008: 304). This, she continues, problematically portrays young-people as incompetent at everything, and adults as competent at everything. Conversely, the 'being' child is presented as an agent of his or her own social world, but this is equally not without difficulties; subverting the possibility of 'becoming' and maintaining the competence and hierarchy of adults. Attempts to integrate both concepts acknowledge the interdependency of children and adults as always being and always becoming, on a journey together (Lee 2001). James et al. (1998) argue that such deeply embedded and time-orientated structures serve to control and limit young-people's lives but equally and paradoxically emerge as sites of agency, possibility and experience.

These and many other ways, construct children as different from adults. In the West, childhood is romanticised and sentimentalised; the child depicted as innocent, future, lacking in knowledge and understanding, and always in contrast to the all-knowing adult. Arguably, these distinctions are becoming less discernible, and in a similar way to the life/death boundary, the adult/child one is blurring. These changes and uncertainties have given rise to the argument that childhood, having gradually emerged as a separate category to adulthood from the thirteen century onwards, is now disappearing. Postman, in his book *The Disappearance of Childhood* (1982), contends that the dividing line between adult and child is wearing thin and points to childhood as an 'endangered species' (1982: 4). He contends that the unrestricted opening up of 'dark and fugitive mysteries' (1982: 87), such as mental illness, homosexuality and specifically in this case death, pose dangers to the continuation of childhood. The worries and anxieties created by such thinking are, Prout contends, the result of structuring variations between adult and childhood as 'historically progressive and even necessary' (2005: 14) and pointing the finger of blame firmly at new technologies, which provide a wide range of previously unavailable and potentially 'damaging' information to young-people. Conversely, the opposing view envisages information technology as the saviour of childhood by overturning 'generational hierarchies and liberating children from outdated social forms' (Prout 2005: 14). Neither position offers a full reading of the situation, nor considers the diversity of childhoods, or the complexity of young-people's interactions with technology and their lived experiences. Consequently, the defined lines and assumptions of knowledge and power are less clear and the predicted journey to adulthood is less certain, if achievable at all.

The New Sociology of Childhood

The new sociology of childhood, now arguably not so new, established itself during the 1980s and 1990s within the oppositional debates and dichotomous arguments of modernist sociology and social theory, such as structure versus agency, local versus global, continuity versus change and so on. A period of rapid structural and institutional changes compelled social theory to search for new approaches and it was within these changing dimensions that the contemporary sociology of childhood had its beginnings. The problem for the new sociology of childhood was that sociology in general, with a few exceptions, had provided little room within its confines for childhood. Therefore, it had to create space not only for childhood within sociological discourse but also confront the complexity of childhood as a new and pluralistic phenomenon. What was considered novel about the new approach was a determination to make 'childhoods' the focus of concern, rather than subsume the child under topics such as the family or school (James et al. 1998). However, the brave-new-world of the freely exploring, socially participatory child was almost over before it had begun. Jenks claiming that, 'a gerontocratic hegemony, policed by discipline, and legitimised through ideologies of care, protection and privacy' (2005: 74–75), formed impenetrable barriers.

However, as Gittins (1998) points out, children did not and still do not live in a vacuum, they are not separate from the rest of society. Whilst traditional aspects of socialisation focus on the child's internalisation of adult skills and knowledge, more recently, Corsaro points to a more collaborative approach; 'interpretive reproduction' (2011: 20). From this perspective, children rather than being passive recipients, play an innovative and creative role in which they actively appropriate information from the adult world to address their own peer concerns. The 'interweaving' of adult/child worlds, as suggested above, is important to the consideration of end-of-life discussions, it has the potential to enrich the lives/deaths of children and adults alike and contribute to the production of cultural and social change.

Therefore, the new sociology of childhood and ensuing debates call into question the practice of privileging adult views over those of children, and subsequent literature promotes interacting directly *with* children in order to encourage their participation in research (Fraser et al. 2004; Green and Hogan 2005; Greig et al. 2007; Christensen and James 2008). Research which encourages children to express their views may have little appeal to those who have power over them. However, the public prominence now given to children and their rights in Western societies has challenged conventional thinking and in the process has brought children's perspectives to the fore (Hill 2005).

It would seem reasonable therefore, to suggest that 'traditional ways of representing childhood no longer seem adequate to its emerging forms' (Prout 2005: 7). Children are 'different from the innocent and dependent creatures that appeared to populate the first half of the twentieth century' (Prout 2005: 7). Long established debates, which set biology and developmental psychology in contention with social and culturally constructed vistas of childhood are narrow and tired, allowing only dispassionate views of the child as either being or becoming, innocent or imbued with 'original sin', active or passive, problematic or disappearing but always as 'other than' the omnipresent, omnipotent adult. Consequently, the sociology of childhood and the reconceptualization of children must move on.

Childhood is clearly a multifaceted phenomenon and as Prout (2005) suggests, it is the intermingling of assorted perspectives which provide a more coherent picture of the lives of children and young-people. In concluding this section, I ask what this newly emerging and complex picture of childhood might tell us, especially in relation to mortality. Wall speculates that 'childhood faces humanity with its own deepest and most perplexing questions' (2010: 1), and argues that by examining childhood we can explore life itself; its purpose, its hopes, its aims and paradoxically its endings. Nonetheless, Wall's position is not common-place, and Jenks proposes that adults continue to assume that children are of 'a special order' (2005: 6), and anyone tampering with these fundamental values might be seen to contaminate the world of childhood, endangering those within, and bring down on themselves accusations of sacrilege, blasphemy and profanity. As a result, we must question if the adult conceptualisation of children and childhood has travelled far from its cradle. If childhood remains 'special' then its sacred and hallowed nature, cannot, must not and surely should not be associated with the contamination and profanity of death. Why would anyone do this and heap such opprobrium on their head.

Space for Both Death and Childhood

The literature reviewed thus far demonstrates the complex and changing positions of death and childhood in society, academic thought and subsequently everyday life. That both have, at times, been hidden and marginalised is clear, yet despite this absence they now make frequent appearances throughout societal and academic contexts. Notwithstanding the scholarship identified in these two seemingly separate fields of enquiry, I suggest that a combined space is limited, especially when the universality of death and the proportion of children in relation to the population as a whole, is considered. Only partial attempts have been made to unite the two, arguably creating a new area of sequestration, which denies the knowledge that young-people can bring to this particular table. I contend that despite arguments, which support the blurring of boundaries between life and death, and a similar discussion between childhood and adulthood that a significant boundary persists between death and youth. Higgens states that 'death is a part of children's lives, let's not pretend it is not' (1999: 82), but despite this clear assertion, it seems that to some extent societal, parental and adult views remain opposed to it. How then can Kastenbaum and Fox's (2007) suggestion that adults assume children do not, cannot and should not think about death, and James' claim that children 'are not, should not and cannot be set apart from adults' (2010: 494), be reconciled?

Death and childhood have often shared the same space, and arguably beyond the confines of modern Western society, for millions of children, they still do. The highest rates of child mortality remain in sub-Saharan Africa, where 1 in 12 children die before the age of 5 (United Nations Inter-Agency Group for Child Mortality Estimation 2015); equally experiencing the death of parents and siblings remains prevalent. Historically, encounters with death for children were relatively common, the deaths of family members, often-other children, were an everyday occurrence (Beit-Hallahmi 2011). Gillis (1997) notes that prior to the nineteenth century, children in Western countries, were introduced to death early, death was as familiar to children as to adults, children played death games, built pretend coffins and were conspicuous in their involvement with funerals, wakes and deathbed scenes. Similarly, Ariès (1981/2008) describes how, in the mid seventeenth century, children from Paris orphanages, foundling homes and charity schools were used to escort the funeral processions of the wealthy, he describes these children as, 'specialists in death' (1981/ 2008: 167). However, in more recent times he suggests that children have become excluded from death and are either uniformed or told their loved ones have either 'gone away' or been taken by Jesus. Jesus, he contends 'has become a kind of Santa Claus whom adults use to tell children about death without believing in him themselves' (Ariès 1981/2008: 576).

Although now 20 years ago and clearly culturally apposite, Gillis (1997) also identifies an embargo on children and death, citing medicalisation as a reason for the exclusion of children from the deathbed, their exemption from taking part in rituals related to the corpse and a gradual removal from funerals all together. More recently, Beit-Hallahmi concurs, asserting that contemporary mortality clearly dissociates itself 'from the physical events of dying, death and the disposal of dead bodies' (2011: 42), through distancing, anonymity and professionalisation. These modern 'ideals' are presented to young-people raising concerns about a culture which arguably goes to 'extraordinary efforts to hide the reality of death from children' (Beit-Hallahmi 2011: 42). Under such circumstances, 'the child had become the favourite symbol of life' (Gillis 1997: 210).

Perspectives on Death and Childhood

However, notwithstanding the controversy detailed above, children's understanding of death has been explored. Hunter and Smith (2008) acknowledge that the development of such an enterprise occurred steadily over the last 60 years and that a large body of work, predominantly arising from the perspective of developmental psychology, has been concerned with the process by which the child attains a 'mature' concept of death. The understanding of three sub-concepts; universality, irreversibility and nonfunctionality have traditionally been central to this endeavour, and consequently 'age and stage' accounts have been dominant. From this perspective, a 'mature' concept of death gradually evolves through developing cognition. However, this approach is not without criticism. Children's understanding of death does not always follow such a neat progression. Bluebond-Langer and DeCicco highlight the 'sophisticated understanding of death' (2006: 85–86) demonstrated by some young-people, in comparison with the 'childish notions' of some adults. McCormick (2011) equally questions the notion of a 'mature' concept of death, and agrees that adults are often as confused about death as children arguably are. Beit-Hallahmi (2011) identifies a societal expectation that children from any culture should understand the finality, universality and irreversibility of death by the age of twelve, unless serious cognitive disabilities prevent this, and equally suggests that the achievement of such understanding should be considered a developmental milestone and celebrated as other childhood attainments are. And yet, he suggests, 'learning about death is never celebrated, and teaching about death is always done with a heavy heart'; both being marked by 'ambivalence, anxiety, confusion and denial' (2011: 45).

Then again, exploring the literature has uncovered some, if few, notable exceptions, which delve more deeply into the lived experiences of young-people and attempt to promote their views and voices more strongly. One highly noteworthy example is the seminal work of Myra Bluebond-Langner, *The Private Worlds of Dying Children* (1978), and her pioneering inclusion of children's views and experiences. The findings, although now nearly 40-years-old, remain highly relevant to the continued reluctance of adults to discuss death with children.

Bluebond-Langer directly engaged with dying children at a time when opinion suggested that because these children did not ask adults about it they were unaware of the gravity of their situation. The children in question had a diagnosis of leukaemia, a disease that at the time presented very little hope of recovery and potentially, imminent death. Bluebond-Langer, positioned children as 'wilful, purposeful individuals capable of creating their own world' (1978: 7) and credited them with understanding and the ability to interpret and deduce events going on around them. In contrast, the adults; parents, nurses, doctors, failed to recognise the child's complex and profound understanding of their illness and mortality. Paradoxically then, these young-people considered that talking to adults about death was inappropriate, as adults never talked to them about it. However, it was a topic of conversation they considered appropriate with other children, evidenced by their willingness to offer information and answer questions. It was clear that despite limited or no discussion with them about the severity of their illness and its ultimate consequences, children were aware of their poor prognosis and the inevitability of death; however, they hid this knowledge from parents and other adults. This act of 'mutual pretence' Bluebond-Langer contends, is a device to maintain socially prescribed roles and responsibilities threatened by terminal illness and death; parent as nurturer, doctor as curer, child as future. As an example of the importance of time, structure and generation to societal constructions of childhood, the lived experiences of young-people whose time is limited by terminal illness are an anathema. Here the inevitability of death collides with the monolith of childhood futurity, dying children positioned, if not outside of the realm of childhood, then in some liminal, betwixt-and-between space. Bluebond-Langer illustrates this ambiguity, in which dying children resemble more closely older-people rather than their peers, not only in their appearance—bald, emaciated, sickly, but equally in their lack of future and increased worries and responsibility for the feelings of others. Most of all Bluebond-Langer contends, these children are 'failing with time' and 'Their worth can only be measured by what they do now, unlike other children, who have time to prove themselves' (1978: 213).

Bluebond-Langer's work demonstrates that mutual pretence and silence between adults and young-people in relation to death maintains the social order, upholds the status quo and challenges nothing, leaving everything as it should be, silent and unsaid. The children in her research were not only aware of their own mortality but that adults saw them as unknowing, innocent and belonging to a future they would never have. Therefore, they kept their information to themselves by acknowledging that adults wished to protect them, and so they protected the 'grown-ups' in return. They recognised the reluctance of adults to discuss death with them as an inappropriate topic for children, and they kept quiet to maintain the social order rather than risk loneliness and abandonment. Surely there is sufficient evidence here to give all young-people the opportunity to be listened to, on their own terms, in relation to death. Bluebond-Langer argues, that the 'practice of mutual pretence reflects a human dilemma far more fundamental than the fear of 'breaking a taboo'—the existential dilemma' (1978: 230). Therefore, the on-going voyage to uncover the rich, sophisticated and diverse relationship between death and youth continues.

In response to the context of Bluebond-Langer's work, I wonder if death and youth will only ever be considered in the light of what Ribbens McCarthy calls 'significant biographical events' (2006: 180), that is major bereavements. Research in this sphere is prolific and seeks to theorise grief in a framework of normal and abnormal responses (Kübler Ross 1969/2009; Parkes 1972/1996; Worden 1982). Seale (1998) contends that such approaches are linked to the medicalisation of grief, which aims to illicit 'healthy' rather than pathological outcomes, and serve to 'police' (Walter 1999: 126) or control internal emotions. Whilst an increasing amounts of literature, dedicated to the voice of significantly bereaved children is evident, Ribbens McCarthy (2006) rightly pinpoints a scarcity in potentially less disruptive contexts. This highly singular focus on major loss, she argues, perpetuates a picture of bereavement as only relevant to a minority of young-people. In association, Ribbens McCarthy and Jessop (2005) call for a more 'mainstream' approach, in which a wider range of deaths can be incorporated, for example those of pets or celebrities, and the impact these might have. In agreement, this study gathered such ordinary, everyday and mundane experiences of death, which were nonetheless 'significant' in the lives of these young-people.

Uneasy Conversations

Despite the possibilities suggested above, it seems that death and youth continue to share an uneasy alliance, perhaps due in-part to what Beit-Hallahmi describes as a 'revolution in human existence' (2011: 43). He argues that over the past two centuries biomedicine has 'decisively connected death to old age', thus changing and transforming the way it is thought about and thereby 'sever[ing] the link between childhood and death' (2011: 44). From this perspective, death as a topic of conversation is not necessarily ignored by adults but can certainly be delayed and postponed until they deem the time appropriate. Therefore, despite previous arguments that the death taboo has diminished in Western thinking and that death is a visible entity in a number of ways, Talwar (2011) maintains that death remains a topic we find unpleasant to contemplate and that this is particularly so when children are involved.

Almost 30 years prior to Talwar, Elias noted that 'Nothing is more characteristic of the present day attitude to death than the reluctance of adults to make children acquainted with the facts of death (1985: 18). He points to adult fears, which relate to harming children through knowledge of mortality, as the main reason for the lack of such discussions. Similarly, Bluebond-Langner and DeCicco insist that 'death, like sex, is a topic which adults find difficult to discuss with children' as it is seen to be a 'painful, confusing intrusion into a child's world' (2006: 85). This reticence, they suggest 'assumes that death is foreign to a child's usual thoughts, that it is distressing for a child to even consider, and that it is difficult for him/her to grasp' (2006: 85).

From a broader perspective, Lee (2008) proposes that death remains an improper topic of conversation in a number of places, and as is evident in the literature, it would seem that childhood is definitely one such place. For example, as already noted, Kastenbaum and Fox (2007) highlight adult assumptions that children cannot, do not, and should not think about death, and St Vincent Millais' (1937) poetry further illustrates that 'Childhood is the Kingdom where nobody dies'. In relation to death as a taboo topic for children, Ariès (1974) provides a clear picture of previous generations of children as central to deathbed scenes but kept in the dark about their beginnings. Conversely, contemporary children seem well instructed in the beginning of life, whilst the endings are left well alone. Berridge concurs that 'death is the first big lie parents tell children, a close second to Father Christmas' (2002: 4). She explains, that during her own childhood (she alludes to herself as belonging to the baby boom generation), death was, 'kept at a safe distance by silence and denial', and using the classic children's story of *The Emperor's New Clothes* she illustrates how adults work together to create an illusion of life without death by supressing the desire, unlike the child in the story, to shout it from the roof tops. She affirms that adults 'collude and deny: *carpe diem*, not *memento mori*' (2002: 5).

Sharing Secrets

Higgens claims that, 'If we do not want children to be afraid of death then we must give them the opportunity to discuss the subject' (1999: 85) and Yalom makes the case that, despite adult reticence, young-people do notice deaths presence,

> Children at an early age cannot help but note the glimmerings of mortality surrounding them – dead leaves, insects and pets, disappearing grandparents, grieving parents, endless acres of cemetery tombstones. Children may simply observe, wonder, and following their parents' example, remain silent (2008: 3).

Although Yalom acknowledges, on behalf of young-people, an awareness of death, Piven contends they may equally avoid it by submerging themselves in life and living, leaving the contemplation of death to 'philosophers, poets and melancholics' (2009: 198). Whatever the truth of these arguments, surely young-people may equally treat death with and without awareness at times of their choosing, or at times when it is forced upon them. What is undeniable is that children live in a world of highly prolific and everyday representations of death; TV, roadside memorials, ghost bikes, internet chat rooms, Facebook memorial pages, celebrity deaths, and the widespread use of death that permeates an amount of teenage fiction from Harry Potter to The Hunger Games and beyond. However, exposure to death in childhood is not only via the media. Noppe and Noppe contend that there is a wide acknowledgment that adolescents contemplate their own deaths, encounter the deaths of others and may respond to these in unique ways, however they go on to point out 'a striking lack of empirical research on this topic' (1997: 254). The overarching assumption that knowledge in relation to death is developed via the formation of formal, abstract patterns of thought has, they suggest, brought research in this area to a 'fait accompli' (1997: 254) that resists continued exploration of young-people's conceptions of death.

It is clear that attempts to research children's perceptions of death can be problematic. Developmental psychology has been the most extensive in this area but the imposed theoretical frameworks have arguably closed-down rather than opened-up the topic to wider scrutiny. Young-people live in a world where technology connects them with knowledge more readily than ever before and secrets are hard to keep in an age of readily available information, communication and highly connected networks, both virtual and actual. Postman argues that these better-informed children can no longer be regarded as such and that 'having access to the previously hidden fruit of adult information, they are expelled from the garden of childhood' (1982: 97). Both death, or more precisely visions of an afterlife, and of course childhood, have both been viewed using this garden metaphor. Ariès remarks that 'if the dead slept, it was usually in a garden of flowers' (1981/2008: 25) and Holt, as mentioned previously, imagines childhood within a garden. Perhaps it is pertinent to suggest then, that both might exist happily together within the same garden, sharing their ideas and feelings as and when they arise, without fear of expulsion.

Summary and Moving Forward

The chapter thus far, has fulfilled its aim of reviewing key literature from across the disciplines of death and childhood studies. No one account has been satisfactory in explaining all these complex and dynamic ideas and the evidence produced has often been complex and contradictory. However, the search has revealed a number of illuminating perspectives through which the interconnected nature of both the study of death and the study of childhood have tentatively been glimpsed.

The literature has clearly demonstrated that death is not static in its meanings and that attitudes towards death and dying are 'always amorphous and in flux' (Staudt 2009a: 4). Changes in academic thought and in societal experience have been represented; from death as an everyday and highly collective event to the most feared of individual and existential episodes, via sequestration where death has been both hidden and forbidden, to newly emerging approaches. These latter arguments, offer to release death from its hiding places or at the very least to shine a light into some of the darker recesses in which it has been confined. A possible re-enchantment with death, glimpsed in the literature, offers Western societies' the potential of re-committing to the end-of-life via newly emerging deathways, which can bring it, once again, back into the everyday realm. Death, it seems is in fashion and the literature presented here, and a great deal that is not, concurs with this affirmation.

Similarly, childhood is an equally challenging arena to study as adults preserve, uphold and sustain nostalgic reflections of innocence, futurity and difference. Despite protestations that this way of looking at childhood is outmoded, and that children are knowledgeable, socially active agents with their own participatory rights, some topics are considered threatening and unsuitable for children generally, and death is one of these. As a consequence, there is one area in particular where death is not 'in', and perhaps if not altogether 'out', is kept at a respectable distance, and this is within the realm of childhood.

The similarities and differences between these two arguably disparate areas of study are, I contend, noteworthy. Both death and childhood were once treated as marginalised subjects of enquiry within the discipline of sociology and within society, but have recently emerged into the mainstream. In the public sphere both have been alluded to within the context of sequestration, but both are now highly visible aspects of everyday life. Yet despite this, and children's high levels of exposure to implied or indirect forms of death, the literature continues to attest to adult reluctance to discuss the topic with them. The developmental approach aspires to define the ages and stages at which children acquire a 'mature' concept of death, paving the way for research in this field, and being built upon and extended to include children who have experienced bereavement as a significant life event, and indeed children with a life-limiting condition. Although, some researchers have sought to promote the narrative accounts of children (Bluebond-Langer 1978; Ribbens McCarthy 2006; Fearnley 2012), Alderson argues that 'children and young-people are largely ignored in many adult-centred concerns' (2013: 7), and therefore, I contend, that within this field of enquiry, agendas of theorisation, medicalisation, pathology and 'correct' responses to grief, have remained persistent.

Previously, Elias (1985) has argued that adults need to find a way to talk to children about death, rather than leaving them to their own devices. He argues that the conventions of previous generations appear 'shallow and worn out', 'sound stale and insincere' and 'new rituals reflecting the current standard of feeling and behaviour ... do not exist yet' (1985: 24). Despite this call to action, now 30 years ago, research focusing on the social context of everyday interactions between children and death remains thin on the ground. Children's daily experience brings them into contact with death on a regular basis. They may not have experienced a significant bereavement but nevertheless have knowledge, understanding and experience of death in many other ordinary ways and forms. This potentially deep well of information and understanding needs to be explored, and adult reticence abandoned in order to listen, rather than deny, children and young-people the opportunity to demonstrate their own knowledge, understanding and feelings in relation to this emotive, yet everyday topic.

Proper Conversations?

Having explored, via the presented literature, the vibrant and ever-changing positions of both death and childhood and having witnessed the intricacies and complexities of uniting the two on an ordinary and everyday level, we are still left questioning how to go about eliciting such conversations. It is clear that certain topics, and death is one of these, are positioned as sensitive, barred and off-limits for both young participants and not-so-young researchers alike. Attempts to get this research through an ethics committee and underway was tortuous, due in-part, to the so-called 'sensitivity' [hypersensitivity] surrounding it. To illustrate this delicacy my request to talk to 'children about death' was considered inappropriate but to do the same with 'young-people about the end-of-life' deemed, if slightly eccentric, then at least suitable. The gentler wording perhaps assuaged some of the perceived adult sensitivity. Nevertheless, Milne and Lloyd (2009) contend that assumptions are made that researching the end-of-life must be sensitive because of the deeply personal issues involved. Renzetti and Lee (1993), rather worryingly define a sensitive topic as one that potentially poses a substantial threat to those involved. More reassuringly Hydén suggests that any topic can be deemed sensitive but what is and what is not a sensitive topic is due mainly to the relationship between the 'teller and the listener' (2008: 122). She explains that sensitive topics can be discussed within close relationships, such as friends or family, or within 'special relationships' (2008: 125) such as the doctor-patient, which allow some of the intimacy of the topic to be removed. 'Special relationships' were central to this research, however not ones in which the intimacy of the topic was stripped away as Hydén contends, rather on the contrary, but within the special relationships of the young-people as friends and their relationship with me as the researcher.

After casually overhearing some children discussing the end-of-life with no apparent difficulty, other than a few shocked comments to each other such as 'you can't say that' or 'that's gross', I wondered if young-people viewed this subject as any more sensitive or prohibited than many other everyday topics. I suggest that death is a familiar topic to young-people, and equally that they are competent to discuss it. My response to frequently asked question of 'why discuss end-of-life with young-people' is a considered - why not? However, I acknowledge that this position is open to criticism and could easily be turned into reasons why carrying out this research could be seen as problematic. Throughout this process I have often been asked about the appropriateness of this topic for young-people and in response, I suggest that research with children and young-people has shifted and seeks to include them in more general social enquiry, stepping beyond the boundary of the 'walled garden'. Uprichard (2010) argues that there continues to be a discrepancy between the way in which children are conceptualised in research, as active agents, and the types of research in which they are predominantly involved. She encourages children's involvement in projects that venture beyond the traditional spaces of childhood. It is my hope that this piece of research did just that, by abandoning the demarcated boundaries between death and youth, taking a hands-off approach and trusting in the young-people themselves, enabled the conversations to wander at will and ignite the expert notions that young-people have on this topic. As Uprichard clearly states 'children are capable of talking about many, many things, not just about their childhood lives' [deaths] (2010: 7).

Therefore, after much deliberation and in order to capture these everyday encounters with death, I tentatively stepped in, perhaps where angels fear to tread. I considered the best approach to be qualitative and participatory in nature. Straightforward as this sounds, layers of complexity were involved in order to create an appropriate methodological stance. The philosophies chosen were eclectic and encompassing, utilising ideas from the 'new' paradigm for the sociology of childhood (James and Prout 1997), critical humanism (Plummer 2001), feminist and postmodern approaches. I liken this to a stained glass window, through which the mundane could be illuminated by a variety of phantasmagorical shapes, patterns and colours, the overall effect being, I hoped, a coherent and vibrant picture.

Stepping Through the Stained Glass Window

Denzin and Lincoln (2008) argue that qualitative research belongs to many disciplines, it privileges no single methodological practice, encompasses many theoretical perspectives, and adopts an interpretive, naturalistic approach that attempts to make sense of events in terms of the meanings people bring to them. And yet despite this intricacy they allude to its popularity and 'a quiet methodological revolution', which has drawn the social sciences and the humanities closer together (Denzin and Lincoln 2008: vii). Likewise, I would argue in a similar way to Kvale and Brinkman that, 'If you want to know how people understand their world and their lives, why not ask them'? (2009: xvii). The popularity of the qualitative approach and the 'art of listening' precludes what Back describes as 'thin description or flat sociology bereft of vitalism or life or—I hesitate to write this—any beauty' (2007: 164). Sociology, Back contends, should provide space for things that cannot be said, afford respect for the uncelebrated, champion alternative stories, produce critical and open-minded accounts, and have a desire to listen and take the people we listen to as seriously as ourselves. In so doing, he argues that we may point to a different type of future. These are my hopes for this research.

The qualitative turn is relevant here for a number of reasons. Lee (1993) suggests that qualitative approaches have been deemed the method of choice in sensitive research and Grieg et al. (2007) that they are particularly suitable for research with children. Greene and Hogan highlight attempts to capture the 'richness of experience' (2005: 13) and elevate young-people's voices as the main source of knowledge. Taking a postmodern turn, Dickson-Swift et al. (2008) argue that from this perspective, researchers are not involved in the search for one truth or reality, rather for multiple truths and realities. Liamputtong and Ezzy (2005) emphasise how qualitative research, based on an interpretive paradigm, is exploratory in nature, enabling researchers to gain information about an area in which little is known. Equally, as the researcher begins to share the experiences and meanings of the participants a level of 'sympathetic understanding' (Dickson-Swift et al. 2008: 19) develops, enabling the building of closer relationships, trust and rapport. It was from within this framework of sympathetic understanding, multiple truths, interpretation and exploration that I hoped to learn the views of these young participants and bring their stories to light. Whilst I acknowledged the potential for emotional responses from both the participants and myself, my hope was that this gentle, qualitative and unassuming approach, would allow for the collaborative unfolding and co-construction of ideas via the support and reassurance of friends.

Critical Humanism

So what of the other theoretical approaches mentioned in the introduction to this chapter, those that add to the stained glass window effect and contribute so strongly to the way in which I envisaged chatting with these young-people. First, the work of Plummer whose ideas resonate closely with my own in relation to engaging in human research. Critical humanism focuses and values human experience, utilises ethics of care, compassion and sympathy, evokes respect and trust, and employs a variety of methods to 'bring out the story' (Plummer 2008: 487). Critical humanism goes by many names; 'symbolic interactionism, ethnography, qualitative inquiry, reflexivity, cultural anthropology and life story research', but its focus is 'human subjectivity, experience and creativity' (2008: 482).

In order to capture the essence of complex lives we must recognise that knowledge can only ever be 'limited and partial' (Plummer 2001: 15), and to this end critical humanism has turned to the humanities and the narrative turn for its evidence. The influence of both has developed a softer, warmer, more imaginative style of data collection, its objectives being to interpret, describe and appreciate, rather than the harder and colder approach of scientific sociology, whose aim is to measure and theorise (Plummer 2001: 9). Plummer suggests that researchers take a different view and apply diverse research methods, such as 'photography, art, video, film, poetics, drama, narrative' (2008: 496), or even as used here, 'stuff in a box'. Plummer (2008) asserts that contemporary humanistic research methods can enlighten our understanding of other people's lives, and here I add deaths.

The central tenets of critical humanism, as described above, suggested my way forward. The human being, the young-person as central to this research, the value and valuing of that person and their experiences, the multiple ways in which they might tell their stories, the different influences on their narratives, the inclusion of art, literature, material culture, my own interpretations of the data, reflexivity, subjectivity and an ethic of care, all spoke of partial but colourful ways of seeing.

Feminism

Allen and Walker (1992) contend that feminism is a perspective, an epistemology and an ontology, a way of seeing, knowing and being in the world and therefore, in a similar way to Plummer's humanism, it was useful in shaping a caring and supportive approach. Just as feminist research challenged the traditional social order and opened up possibilities for women, Cockburn argues that feminism has generated a unique set of ideas that have 'important repercussions for the sociological study of childhood' (2005: 72). Crucially, feminist researchers have successfully studied issues that are controversial or laden with emotion by rejecting the traditional separation of the researcher and the researched and setting goals of consciousness raising and empowerment (Renzetti and Lee 1993). The adoption of feminist principles, for example non-hierarchical relationships, care and concern for participants, acknowledging my own personal involvement in the subjective nature this work, were all central to carrying it out. A feminist approach is analogous with, and has laid the foundations for, research with children and young-people, and was essential and pivotal to engaging with young-people on this topic.

'New' Sociology of Childhood

Young-people are central to this research in order to capture how things are for them. There has been a long tradition of research involving children dating back to the beginning of the twentieth century; frequently within this context the child was conceptualised as 'incompetent, unreliable and incomplete' (Barker and Weller 2003: 208), and their lives scrutinised from the perspectives of adults (Christianson and James 2008). Derbyshire et al. (2005) observe that researchers undertaking qualitative research with children confront a variety of perspectives, among them cultural, social, psychological and political, which situate the child as less than competent and therefore incapable of being taken seriously.

However, over the past 20 years, and in particular the last ten, there has been a rapid expansion in the sociological study of children's lives

(Mayall 2002). The 1990s saw the inclusion of ideas from 'the new social studies of childhood', the United Nations Convention on the Rights of the Child (UNCRC 1989) and the UK Children's Act (1989), all of which began to challenge adult thinking about children and childhood, viewing the young as competent social actors, whose lives are worthy of investigation. Children became the subjects rather than the objects of academic exploration, and research carried out 'with' rather than previously 'on' children. Roberts (2004) emphasised the importance of UNCRC articles 12 and 13 in advocating that a child has a right to his or her own views and to express them freely, thus ascribing an entitlement to participate in discussions and decisions and therefore their voices to be heard. Thompson (2008) supports the view that children and young-people are capable of providing expert testimony about their experiences and an ability to offer unique insights into their everyday lives. Notwithstanding such assured views, is Lahman's (2008) acknowledgment that the young can be both competent and vulnerable at the same time, a notion particularly worthy of consideration here. Surely however, this is no less a pertinent point when discussing death with adults.

The combination of these perspectives, critical humanism, feminist standpoints and more recent approaches to researching young-people, whilst eclectic and not without criticism, helped to guide my beliefs and actions through this research. Weaving these ideas together calls to mind Denzin and Lincoln's (2008) suggestion that the qualitative researcher is a bricoleur, a jack-of-all-trades, who uses all available tools to create a bricolage, a montage, a piecing together of odds and ends, creating multiple images that continually develop and emerge into new meanings and new representations, ultimately making a cohesive whole. The culmination of the bricoloeur's work is 'a complex, dense, reflexive collage like creation that represents the researcher's images, understandings, and interpretations of the world' (Mcleod 1996: 72).

Qualitative research of this type faces many criticisms and challenges, being condemned as soft science, exploratory rather than factual, subjective rather than objective, criticism rather than theory, and lacking in objective value free truth (Denzin and Lincoln 2008). The qualitative researcher's response, and therefore mine, lies within an interpretative framework, exploring a world of lived experience, utilising descriptive materials and advocating active participation. These core beliefs, drawn from a variety of methodological paradigms, underpinned how I would approach this project. Influenced centrally by the human being at its core, the socially active and competent child, the relationship between the listener and the teller, and an ethic of care. Aware of the emotional potential, I considered this qualitative, interpretative, experiential structure appropriate. Within this framework the researcher needs to acknowledge their own values, beliefs and emotions in order to interact fully with their participants. Such reflexivity requires, Guba and Lincoln suggest, that the researcher come to terms not only with the research question and those involved, but with the different selves brought to and developed within the research, leading to a process of 'discovery of the subject', and furthermore a 'discovery of the self' (2008: 27).

Participation and Putting 'Stuff' in a Box

Having located these philosophical perspectives, I feel it is similarly valuable to consider the methods that reinforced them. The following section explores these, looking in more detail at how focus groups as a data collection method and collecting 'stuff in a box' were used to develop conversations and interactions between the participants and myself. In response to Katz's contention that there is a 'paucity of knowledge of what children of different ages understand about death' (2001: 145), the choice of age group and equally methods, which could potentially assist and encourage the telling of stories, took time to consider.

The UNCRC (1989) defines a child as any human being under the age of 18 years, and therefore I initially identified an age range of young-people between ten and seventeen to sit within these chronological boundaries. My selection was due in part to developmental arguments, which suggest that the cognitive understanding of the universality and permanency of death are present at this age (Nagy 1948; Kenyon 2001). However, it was not my intention to situate cognitive developmental arguments as the central tenets upon which to build this study. I did not wish to imply that the understanding of death is situated within narrow age related boundaries, and proceeds in an orderly and linear fashion towards a 'mature' understanding, which arguably excludes any possibility of extraordinary or 'magical thinking'. Instead, it was the inclusion of a variety of life experiences and a range of stories, that was central to my choice of age range. From a purely pragmatic approach the wide age range allowed for greater flexibility and likewise acknowledged the uncertainty of who might wish to volunteer.

Focus Groups

The choice to use focus groups, made up of friends, was an attempt to provide a familiar context within the unfamiliar circumstances of research, thereby creating a more relaxed environment, which would facilitate unrestrained conversation. I considered a group approach, rather than one-to-one interviews, would aid in transferring the balance of power from myself and rather disseminate it amongst the participants. This I feel, played a vital role in providing and sustaining interactive opportunities that were less influenced and controlled by me and more readily opened up the topic to vibrant conversation. In consideration of the potential sensitivity and emotionality of the topic, I felt that small groups of between three to six participants would generate a friendlier, more intimate, supportive and interactive context. Equally, in relation to the practicalities of group size, I considered that larger groups may not provide equal opportunities for the telling and sharing of stories.

In some respects, I hesitate to use the term 'focus group' to describe the reality of this method. However, I am equally uncertain what alternative term should be used when focus group, in its most basic sense, is a group of people collected together to discuss a particular topic. However, the term lacks the colour, intensity and often humour of the actual conversations and therefore a passing reference to Lewis Carroll's, 'A Mad Tea-Party' in *Alice's Adventures in Wonderland*, better illustrates the actual experience of these group discussions. Similarly, Johannson (2011) argues that rather than adopting the conventional wisdom of sombre researcher asking humourless questions to equally solemn participants, it is preferable to take a relaxed approach. This allows both the researcher and the participants to step out of their designated roles, resulting in 'an encounter beyond age, where the pleasurable practice of laughing and small-talking continues to produce positive relations', thus transforming the encounter from 'knowledge-gaining to entertainment (which does not of course prevent knowledge being produced)' (2011: 108).

Focus groups have become increasingly popular as a means of data collection, despite negative opinions, which situate them as a market research fad of the 1980s (Hollander 2004). Notwithstanding controversy, there is evidence to suggest that they are of value in studying socially marginalised groups and sensitive topics (Liamputtong 2007). Equally, it has been suggested that they are particularly suitable for use with young-people as they create a safe peer environment that replicates familiar social groups (Mauthner 1997) and enables young-people to 'feel empowered and supported in the co-presence of those they know' (Morgan et al. 2002: 17). Lewis goes further and contends that 'friendship patterns' (1992: 418) may be the most important factor for composing these groups. Moreover, Hollander (2004) suggests that focus groups are useful as they allow the researcher-role to be played down and the participants' voices to come to the fore, thereby acknowledging the participants as experts. The role of the adult is therefore to facilitate the young-people's participation within the group so that they do not feel that they are being questioned but are indeed sharing ideas, views and experiences with a set of peers (Hennessy and Heary 2005).

Focus groups have been criticised for the problems researchers face in regulating the group dynamic and dealing with the more outspoken members who attempt, and may succeed, in dominating conversations (Hesse-Biber and Leavy 2011). Arguably, as focus groups membership was organised by the young-people themselves and established on the basis of friendship then interactive conversations developed readily. The ability of members to listen attentively, act supportively, express their feelings 'in their own words', and in certain instances tell each other to 'shut up' was beneficial. As Derbyshire et al. suggest, 'Research with children demands flexibility' (2005: 423) and the ability to 'go with the flow' (2005: 421), this they contend is not 'sloppy methodology' but an important element in this type of research.

Upon reflection, an amusing lesson learned is not to provide biscuits with foil wrappers as a source of refreshment during the recording of focus group interactions. Pizza, cups of tea and coffee, party ring biscuits (a particular favourite it seems) and various cakes help to provide a positive environment for discussion and are no hindrance to the later interpretation of data. However, a tendency amongst the participants to smooth out the foil packaging once the contents of certain biscuits have been consumed can make listening to the recorded conversations an interesting challenge.

'Stuff' in a Box

In order to capture experiences, Punch suggests that carrying out research with young-people may require the 'creation of innovative techniques or the adaptation of traditional ones' (2002: 45). Likewise, Lahman concurs that it is an interesting time to become involved in researching children and young-people when 'the use of innovative research methods are burgeoning' (2008: 293). However, both provide words of caution. In contrast to traditional methods of enquiry, participatory methods may be more interesting and rewarding for the young-people involved but they should not be used just for the sake of it. Therefore, after lengthy consideration I found myself inspired by the use of memory boxes; often promoted by bereavement charities as a therapeutic intervention for young-people, in which small objects and reminders of a person who has died are collected together. As young-people in this study were not specifically chosen because they had experienced bereavement, although many had, I asked them to collect 'stuff' (Miller 2010), 'the 'stuff' of everyday life' (Hockey et al. 2010: 7), objects that evoked ideas, feelings, beliefs and relationships with death. The items were placed in shoeboxes, [the local shoe shop was more than happy for me to take them] and brought along to the discussions. In so doing, traditional and participatory methods were merged. The young-people having engaged with the collection of items prior to the group conversations were more than ready to take part in conversations.

Nothing could have prepared me for the fascinating array of objects. There was a plentiful assortment of books, films and computer games. Equally, a variety of treasured mementoes belonging to deceased friends and relatives; Granddad's swimming medals, Uncle Charlie's ceramic blue dolphin, Grandma's bell, and even Granddad's ashes with an accompanying death certificate. There were photographs, tissues, candles, orders of service, poems read at funerals and a black shirt worn by one young man at his Grandma's funeral. More obscure objects included a USB cable, a bunch of keys, a pair of tweezers and a tin of sweet corn. The most frequently included object, both physically and in representational form was the knife, often associated and discussed within the context of violent death. Some of the young-people made the box into a work of art, painting them and sticking words, song lyrics, pictures of coffins and religious symbols both on and inside the box, or filling it with words cut from newspapers and magazines. Two participants painted their boxes, both black. One of whom explained that her box was black on the outside to represent death and look like a coffin, but on the inside it was a vivid blue and sprinkled with glitter suggesting, she explained, that death is often represented as bad and dark, but in contrast it can be seen as good, depicted by the blue and the glitter. The objects acted as a starting point, a platform from which ideas and feelings could begin to be uncovered. This powerful collection of objects provided a stimulus for the telling of personal stories, expressions of feelings, discussions, exchange of ideas, jokes, laughter and quiet reflective moments. Punch (2002) mentions how such stimulus materials can act as prompts and enable ideas to be expanded upon. This was certainly the case here.

The use of 'stuff' provided fertile ground for conversations, and since material objects often help in 'making sense of death' (Hockey et al. 2010a: 6) their presence was powerful. Whilst Miller (2010) contends that the tem 'stuff' is difficult to define, he equally suggests that the term 'material culture' is no easier but helps by arguing that 'material culture thrives as a rather undisciplined substitute for a discipline: inclusive, embracing, original, sometimes quirky researches and observations' (2010: 1). I rather enjoy this definition and suggest that via the use of materiality this study embraced the undisciplined, inclusive and quirky and in so doing identified with the predominantly teenage participants.

To delve a little deeper into this Hockey et al. argue that 'the embodied experiences of the 'stuff 'of everyday life are…pressed into metaphoric service to help make sense of more mysterious or abstract domains' (2010: 7). This, I feel, helps to explain how the interactions between the young-people and the objects, although everyday and often mundane, helped to expose and explore death in greater detail. The objects frequently exemplified previous but nevertheless ongoing relationships with dead loved ones, memorials to relatives, friends and pets, or were used as metaphors to explain concepts such as loss or the collective death of all people. Sometimes they symbolised scientific or religious thinking, represented death rituals, or provided insights into individual or shared experiences. The links between the objects, death and the young-people were central to letting death both physically and metaphorically out of these boxes. As Miller suggests 'stuff is as much a matter of death as it is of life' (2010: 145). Both mundane and prized, this 'stuff' authorised the externalising of ideas, feelings and experiences and gave voice to both new and shared insights into the position of death in the lives of these young-people. Miller and Parrott argue that material objects have often been used as a form of 'gradual divestment and separation' (2009: 503) from the dead. In contrast, these objects acted as a source of investment and contact with the dead, uniting youth, death, sensitivity and materiality.

Ethics

By situating a discussion of ethics at the end of this chapter it is not my intention to consider ethical issues as an afterthought. On the contrary, the ethical and moral musings with which I began this work, reflected my approach to life, to the people I encounter, and to this undertaking. They were not optional, superfluous or added but deeply and personally felt values, which embraced the significance of friendship, sharing, listening, caring and interdependency. They shaped our ability, that is the participants and myself, to 'chat death stuff' with boldness, deference, passion and humour.

Despite changing assumptions about children and childhood, conducting research with young-people continues to raise numerous ethical concerns, which require consideration. The omnipresent concerns of informed consent, anonymity, participants right to withdraw and so on, continue to dominate. Much has been written about these well-established instructions and they will not be re-drawn here. In accordance, Grbich argues that traditional grand narratives, which focus on the blind following of rules in relation to canonical aspects of research, should be regarded with scepticism, emphasising instead 'individually responsible research and respect for others' (2004: 90). Moreover, Plummer (2008) insists that research begins with people and therefore the researcher has a moral and ethical obligation to care, value and respect the individual. Alderson (2004) points out that over the past 30 years ethical standards in research with children have changed considerably and are now based, to a great extent, on transparency, respect and a moral relationship with the participants. Undertaking research on sensitive issues, particularly with children, can raise problems, and therefore Young and Barrett advise the adoption of 'ethical research … predicated on the expectation that the participants will suffer no harm' (2001: 130).

Not wanting to cause any distress but equally not wanting to stop or inhibit displays of emotionality was indeed challenging, both practically and ethically. The potential for this study to generate emotions, both from the participants and for myself, was clearly evident and therefore 'caring' for each other was essential. Tronto perceives care as 'a central but devalued aspect of human life', and that 'To care well involves engagement in an ethical practice of complex moral judgements' (1993/2009: 157). I similarly regard care, both conceptually and practically, as an overlooked, underrated and underestimated aspect of research, and therefore made it pivotal to the ethical and moral success of this project. The informal arrangements of the discussion groups, the conversational approach, the choice by the young-people of which stories to tell, the relaxed context, the inclusion of friends, relationships and connectedness helped to ensure that care was paramount. In Tronto's words 'caring is not just a cerebral concern, or a character trait, but the concern of living, active humans engaged in the processes of everyday living. Care is both a practice and a disposition' (1993/2009: 104). The caring ethos combined with and encouraged further the agency, competence and confidence of these young-people and thus offers an authentic view of their relationship with death, one than has previously gone largely unnoticed.

Hoarding all these ideas together like a magpie, further illuminated the stained-glass window. The values discussed above, have meaning for me and were therefore the ethical foundations upon which this research was built. I can only support Dickson-Swift et al. in their suggestion that undertaking qualitative research is a subjective experience and the researcher cannot 'hide behind the mask of objectivity and pretend they are not intimately involved in the research that they do' (2008: 22–23), because I was and still am. They continue by suggesting the researcher is 'the data collection instrument' (2008: 23) and therefore must directly interact with fellow human beings face-to-face, develop relationships, invest a part of themselves in the data collection, and not be embarrassed by their own subjectivity. Whilst it has been argued that 'care' is undervalued in the context of life and research, contemporaneously Dickson-Swift et al. contend that so is subjectivity. Research that includes such open reflexivity being described as 'contaminated' by the researcher's views. Being subjective, reflecting on my own beliefs and prejudices, and reporting on the personal details involved in this study have, I contend, brought this study to life, an apt description considering the subject matter.

Summary

The methodological stance taken and the methods chosen were, I argue, fit for purpose. Foremost, was the centrality of young-people's views. The informality of each discussion group, giving them an opportunity to tell their own stories in their own ways. The narratives and topics discussed were not shaped or constrained by me as 'the researcher', or by a framework of pre-set questions but emerged individually and converged jointly in a process of sharing, revising, shaping and co-constructing ideas. The ethic of care, of doing no harm, of treading carefully and letting narratives, feelings and openness emerge from the already established relationships, and my inclusion in these, was at the heart of this endeavour. My position as researcher, I argue, was played with a light touch, to some extent hidden under the roles of tea maker, biscuit provider, after school listener, and 'mother-type' role. All of the above, allowed for a free exchange of ideas and for the association of end-of-life as an improper topic of conversation in the context of youth, to be recast as appropriate and apposite.

Conclusion

This chapter has provided a stage on which both youth and death have played many parts. The two main protagonists are not changeless but always shifting, varying and transforming. However, despite their chimera like qualities they are endowed with very definite characters; the youth as vulnerable but nevertheless destined for the future with all its possibilities … sacred, and death as malevolent, threatening to youth's opportunities and potential … profane. In every practical sense they cannot share the same stage, or inhabit the same world, but they can and do, not always in obvious ways. However, in order to become better acquainted with their shared domains it is necessary to carefully and thoughtfully lift the trap-door and release what waits beneath. The stage is then set and the time is right to raise the curtain on the sometimes conventional, often unusual but always though provoking scenes in which death and youth act together.

References

Alderson, P. (2004). Ethics. In S. Fraser, V. Lewis, S. Ding, M. Kellett, & C. Robinson (Eds.), *Doing research with children and young-people*. London: Sage.

Alderson, P. (2013). *Childhoods real and imagined: Volume 1: An Introduction to critical realism and childhood studies*. Abingdon: Routledge.

Allen, K., & Walker, A. (1992). A feminist analysis of interviews with elderly mothers and their daughters. In J. Gilgun, K. Daly, & G. Handel (Eds.), *Qualitative methods in family research*. CA: Sage.

Ariès, P. (1962). *Centuries of childhood: A social history of family values*. London: Jonathan Cape.

Ariès, P. (1974). *Western attitudes towards death: From the middle ages to the present*. London: Marion Boyars.

Ariès, P. (1981/2008) *The hour of our death* (2nd ed.). New York: Vintage.

Back, L. (2007). *The art of listening*. Oxford: Berg.

Barrie, J. M. (1911/1988). *Peter Pan*. London: Methuen Children's Books.

Barker, J., & Weller, S. (2003). Never work with children? The geography of methodological issues in research with children. *Qualitative Research, 3*(2), 207–227.

Bauman, Z. (1992). Survival as a social construct. *Theory, Culture and Society, 9*, 1–13.

Becker, E. (1973). *The denial of death*. New York: The Free Press.

Beit-Hallahmi, B. (2011). Ambivalent teaching and painful learning: Mastering the facts of life (?). In V. Talwar, P. Harris, & M. Schleifer (Eds.), *Children's understanding of death: From biological to religious conceptions*. New York: Cambridge University Press.

Berger, P., & Luckman, T. (1967/1991). *The Social construction of reality: A treatise in the sociology of knowledge*. London: Penguin.

Berridge, K. (2002). *Vigor Mortis*. London: Profile Books.

Bluebond-Langer, M. (1978). *The private worlds of dying children*. Princeton: Princeton University Press.

Bluebond-Langer, M., & DeCicco, A. (2006). Children's views of death. In A. Goldman, R. Hain, & S. Liben (Eds.), *The Oxford textbook of palliative care for children* (2nd ed.). Oxford: Oxford University Press.

Burman, E. (2008). *Deconstructing developmental psychology* (2nd ed.). London: Routledge.

Christensen, P., & James, A. (Eds.). (2008). *Research with children: Perspectives and practices* (2nd ed.). Abingdon: Routledge.

Cockburn, T. (2005). Children and the feminist ethic of care. *Childhood, 12*(1), 71–89.

Corsaro, W. A. (2011). *The sociology of childhood* (3rd ed.). London: Sage.

Davies, C. (2010). Technological taxidermy: Recognisable faces in celebrity deaths. *Mortality, 15*(2), 138–153.

Denzin, N., & Lincoln, Y. (Eds.). (2008). *The landscape of qualitative research*. London: Sage.

Derbyshire, P., MacDougall, C., & Schiller, W. (2005). Multiple methods in qualitative research with children: More Insight or just more? *Qualitative Research, 5*(4), 417–436.

Dickson-Swift, V., James, E. L., & Liamputtong, P. (2008). *Undertaking sensitive research in the health and social sciences: Managing boundaries, emotions and risk*. Cambridge: Cambridge University Press.

Elias, N. (1939/2000). *The civilizing process: Sociogenic and psychogenic investigations*, Revised Edition. Oxford: Blackwell.

Elias, N. (1985). *The loneliness of the dying*. New York: Continuum.

Faulkner, J. (2011). *The importance of being innocent: Why we worry about children*. Port Melbourne: Cambridge University Press.

Fearnley, R. (2012). *Communicating with children when a parent is at the end-of-life*. London: Jessica Kingsley.

Foltyn, J. L. (2008). Dead famous and death sexy: Popular culture, forensics, and the rise of the corpse. *Mortality, 13*(2), 153–173.

Fraser, S., Lewis, V., Ding, S., Kellett, M., & Robinson, C. (Eds.). (2004). *Doing research with children and young-people*. London: Sage.

Giddens, A. (1991). *Modernity and self-identity: Self and society in the late modern age*. Cambridge: Polity Press.

Gillis, J. R. (1997). *A world of their own making: Myth, ritual, and the quest for family values*. Cambridge MA: Harvard University Press.

Gittings, C. (2009). The art of dying. In A. Kellahear (Ed.), *The study of dying: From autonomy to transformation*. Cambridge: Cambridge University Press.

Gittins, D. (1998). *The child in question*. London: Macmillan.

Gorer, G. (1955, October). The pornography of death, *Encounter*.

Gorer, G. (1965). *Death, grief and mourning in contemporary britain*. London: Cresset.

Grbich, C. (2004). *New approaches in social research*. London: Sage.

Green, S., & Hogan, D. (Eds.). (2005). *Researching children's experience: Approaches and methods*. London: Sage.

Greig, A., Taylor, J., & MacKay, T. (2007). *Doing research with children* (2nd ed.). London: Sage.

Guba, E., & Lincoln, Y. (2008). Paradigmatic controversies, contradictions, and emerging confluences. In N. Denzin & Y. Lincoln (Eds.), *The Landscape of Qualitative Research*. London: Sage.

Hanusch, F. (2008). Graphic death in the news media: Present or absent? *Mortality, 13*(4), 301–317.

Hanusch, F. (2010). *Representing death in the news: Journalism media and mortality*. Basingstoke: Palgrave Macmillan.

Hennessy, E., & Heary, C. (2005). Exploring children's views through focus groups. In S. Green & D. Hogan (Eds.), *Researching children's experience*. London: Sage.

Hesse-Biber, S. N., & Leavy, P. (2011). *The practice of qualitative research* (2nd ed.). Thousand Oaks, CA: Sage.

Higgens, S. (1999). Death education in the primary school [1]. *International Journal of Children's Spirituality, 4*(1), 77–90.

Hill, M. (2005). Ethical considerations in researching children's experiences. In S. Green & D. Hogan (Eds.), *Researching children's experience: Approaches and methods*. London: Sage.

Hockey, J., Komaromy, C. & Woodthorpe, K. (2010). Materialising absence. In J. Hockey, C. Komaromy & K. Woodthorpe (Eds.), *The matter of death: Space, place and materiality*. Basingstoke: Palgrave MacMillan.

Hollander, J. A. (2004). The social contexts of focus groups. *Journal of Contemporary Ethnography, 33*(5), 602–637.

Holt, J. (1975). *Escape from childhood: The needs and rights of children*. Middlesex: Penguin.

Howarth, G. (2007). *Death and dying: A sociological introduction*. Cambridge: Polity Press.

Hunter, S., & Smith, D. (2008). Predictors of children's understandings of death: age, cognitive ability, death experience and maternal communicative competence. *Omega—Journal of Death and Dying, 57*(2), 143–162.

Hydén, M. (2008). Narrating sensitive topics. In M. Andrews, C. Squire & M. Tamboukou (Eds.), *Doing narrative research*. London: Sage.

James, A. L. (2010). Competition or integration: The next steps in childhood studies. *Childhood, 17,* 485–499.

James, A., Jenks, C., & Prout, A. (1998). *Theorizing childhood*. Cambridge: Polity Press.

James, A., & Prout, A. (Eds.). (1997). *Constructing and reconstructing childhood: Contemporary issues in the sociological study of childhood* (2nd ed.). London: Falmer.

Jenks, C. (1996). *Childhood*. London: Routledge.

Jenks, C. (2005). A new death of childhood. *Childhood, 12*(1), 5–8.

Johansson, B. (2011). Doing adulthood in childhood research. *Childhood, 19*(1), 101–114.

Kastenbaum, R., & Fox, L. (2007). Do imaginary companions die? An exploratory study. *Omega—Journal of Death and Dying. 56*(2), 123–152.

Katz, J. (2001). Supporting bereaved children at school. In J. Hockey, J. Katz, & N. Small (Eds.), *Grief, mourning and death ritual*. Maidenhead: Open University Press.

Kellehear, A. (2007). *A social history of dying*. Port Melbourne: Cambridge University Press.

Kenyon, B. L. (2001). Current research in children's conceptions of death: A critical review. *Omega—Journal of Death and Dying. 43*(1), 63–91.

Knox, S. L. (2006). Death. Afterlife, and the eschatology of consciousness: Themes in contemporary cinema, mortality, *11*(3), 233–252.

Kubler Ross, E. (1969/2009). *On death and dying: What the dying have to teach doctors, nurses, clergy and their own families*. Abingdon: Routledge.

Kvale, S., & Brinkman, S. (2009). *Interviews: Learning the craft of qualitative research interviewing* (2nd ed.). Thousand Oaks, CA: Sage.

Lahman, M. K. E. (2008). Always othered: Ethical research with children. *Journal of Early Childhood Research, 6*(3), 281–300.

Lee, N. (2001). *Childhood and society: Growing up in an age of uncertainty*. Buckingham: Open University Press.

Lee, R. (2008). Modernity, mortality and re-enchantment: The death taboo revisited. *Sociology, 42*(4), 745–759.

Lee, R. M. (1993). *Doing research on sensitive topics*. London: Sage.

Lewis, A. (1992). Group child interviews as a research tool. *British Educational Research Journal, 18*(4), 413–421.

Liamputtong, P. (2007). *Researching the vulnerable*. London: Sage.

Liamputtong, P., & Ezzy, D. (2005). *Qualitative research methods* (2nd ed.). Melbourne: Oxford University Press.

Mauthner, M. (1997). Methodological aspects of collecting data from children: Lessons from three research projects. *Children and Society, 11,* 16–28.

Mayall, B. (2002). *Towards a sociology for childhood: Thinking from children's lives*. Buckingham: Open University Press.

McCormick, M. (2011). Responsible Believing. In V. Talwar, P. L. Harris, & M. Schleifer (Eds.), *Children's understanding of death*. New York: Cambridge University Press.

McInerney, F. (2009). Cinematic visions of dying. In A. Kellehear (Ed.), *The study of dying: From autonomy to transformation*. Cambridge: Cambridge University Press.

McLeod, J. (1996). The humanistic paradigm. In R. Woolfe & W. Dryden (Eds.), *Handbook of counselling psychology*. London: Sage.

McManus, R. (2013). *Death in a global age*. Basingstoke: Palgrave Macmillan.

Mellor, P. A. (1993). Death in high modernity: The contemporary presence and absence of death. In D. Clark (Ed.), *The sociology of death*. Oxford: Blackwell.

Mellor, P. A., & Shilling, C. (1993). Modernity, self-identity and the sequestration of death. *Sociology, 27*(3), 411–431.

Miller, D. (2010). *Stuff*. Cambridge: Polity Press.

Miller, D., & Parrott, F. (2009). Loss and material culture in South London. *Journal of the Royal Anthropological Institute, 15*, 502–519.

Milne, M. J., & Lloyd, C. E. (2009). Keeping the personal costs down: Minimising distress when researching sensitive issues. In S. Earle, C. Komaromy, & C. Bartholomew (Eds.), *Death and dying: A reader*. London: Sage.

Morgan, M., Gibbs, S., Maxwell, K., & Britten, N. (2002). Hearing children's voices: Methodological issues in conducting focus groups with children aged 7–11 years. *Qualitative Research, 2*(1), 5–20.

Nagy, M. (1948). The child's view of death. *Journal of Genetic Psychology, 73*, 3–27.

Noppe, I. C., & Noppe, L. D. (1997). Evolving meanings of death during early, middle, and later adolescence. *Death Studies, 21*, 253–275.

Noys, B. (2005). *The culture of death*. Oxford: Berg.

Parkes, C. M. (1972/1996). *Bereavement: Studies of Grief in Adult Life* (3rd ed.). London: Routledge.

Piven, J. S. (2009). Death, terror, culture, and violence: A psychoanalytic perspective. In M. K. Bartalos (Ed.), *Speaking of death: America's new sense of mortality*. Westport, CT: Praeger Publishers.

Plummer, K. (2001). *Documents of life 2: An invitation to critical humanism*. London: Sage.

Plummer, K. (2008). Critical humanism and queer theory: Living with the tensions. In N. Denzin & S. Lincoln (Eds.), *The landscape of qualitative research* (3rd ed.). London: Sage.

Postman, N. (1982). *The disappearance of childhood*. New York: Vintage Books.

Prout, A. (2005). *The future of childhood: Towards the interdisciplinary study of children*. Abingdon: RoutledgeFalmer.

Punch, S. (2002). Interviewing strategies with young-people: The 'Secret Box', stimulus material and task-based activities. *Children and Society, 16*, 45–56.

Renzetti, C. M., & Lee, R. M. (1993). *Researching sensitive topics*. London: Sage.

Ribbens McCarthy, J. (2006). *Young-people's experiences of loss and bereavement: Towards an interdisciplinary approach*. Berkshire: Open University Press.

Ribbens McCarthy, J., & Jessop, J. (2005). *Young-people, bereavement and loss: Disruptive transmissions?* London: Joseph Rowntree Foundation/National Children's Bureau.

Roberts, R. (2004). Health and Social Care. In S. Fraser, V. Lewis, S. Ding, M. Kellett, & C. Robinson (Eds.), *Doing research with children and young-people*. London: Sage.

Seale, C. (1998). *Constructing death: The sociology of dying and bereavement*. Cambridge: Cambridge University Press.

Stanley, L., & Wise, S. (2011). The domestication of death: The sequestration thesis and domestic figuration. *Sociology, 45*(6), 947–962.

Staudt, C. (2009a). From Concealment to Recognition: The Discourse on Death, Dying and Grief. In M. K. Bartalos (Ed.), *Speaking of death: America's new sense of morality*. Westport, CT: Praeger.

Staudt, C. (2009b). Covering (up?) death: A close reading of time magazine's September 11, 2001, Special Issue. In M. K. Bartalos (Ed.), *Speaking of death: America's new sense of morality*. Westport, CT: Praeger.

Talwar, V. (2011). Talking to children about death in educational settings. In V. Talwar, P. L. Harris, & M. Schleifer (Eds.), *Children's understanding of death*. New York: Cambridge University Press.

St Vincent Millais, E. (1937). *Childhood is the Kingdom Where Nobody Dies*. Retrieved May 28, 2017, from https://www.poets.org/poetsorg/poem/childhood-kingdom-where-nobody-dies.

Taylor, A. (2011). Reconceptualizing the 'Nature' of childhood. *Childhood, 18*(4), 420–433.

Thomson, P. (Ed.). (2008). *Doing visual research with children and young-people*. Abingdon: Routledge.

Tronto, J. C. (1993/2009). *Moral boundaries: A political argument for an ethic of care*. London: Routledge.

UK Children's Act.(1989). Retrieved January 2, 2013, from http://www.legislation.gov.uk/ukpga/1989/41/contents.

United Nations Convention on the Rights of the Child. (1989). Retrieved January 2, 2013, from http://www.un.org/documents/ga/res/44/a44r025.htm.

United Nations Inter-Agency Group for Child Mortality Estimation. (2015). *Levels & Trends in Child Mortality*. Retrieved October 14, 2016, from http://www.childmortality.org/files_v20/download/IGME. Report 2015 child mortality final.pdf.

Uprichard, E. (2008). Children as 'Being and Becomings': Children, childhood and temporality. *Children and Society, 22,* 303–313.

Uprichard, E. (2010). Questioning research with children: Discrepancy between theory and practice? *Children and Society, 24,* 3–13.

Valentine, C. (2006). Academic constructions of bereavement. *Mortality, 11*(1), 57–78.

Wall, J. (2010). *Ethics: In the light of childhood.* Washington, DC: Georgetown University Press.

Walter, T. (1991). Modern death: Taboo or not taboo? *Sociology, 25*(2), 293–310.

Walter, T. (1994). *The Revival of Death.* London: Routledge.

Walter, T. (1999). *On bereavement: The culture of grief.* Buckingham: Open University Press.

Walter, T. (2008a). The sociology of death. *Sociology Compass, 2*(1), 317–336.

Walter, T. (2008b). *The presence of the dead in society.* Paper presented at the conference on death and dying in 18–21c Europe, Alba Iulia, Romania. Retrieved July 22, 2012, from http://www.bath.ac.uk/cdas/research/.

Walter, T. (2009). Jade's dying body: The ultimate reality show. *Sociological Research Online, 14*(5), 3.1. Retrieved May 27, 2011, from http://www.socresonline.org.uk/14/5/1.html.

Walter, T., Hourizi, R., Moncur, W., & Pitsillides, S. (2011). Does the internet change how we die and mourn? *Overview and Analysis, Omega–Journal of Death and Dying, 64*(4), 275–302.

Worden, J. W. (1982). *Grief counselling and grief therapy: A handbook for the mental health practitioner.* New York: Springer.

Wyness, M. (2006). *Childhood and society: An introduction to the sociology of childhood.* Basingstoke: Palgrave Macmillan.

Yalom, I. D. (2008). *Staring at the Sun: Overcoming the dread of death.* London: Piatkus Books.

Young, L., & Barrett, H. (2001). Ethics and participation: Reflections on research with street children. *Ethics, Place and Environment: A Journal of Philosophy and Geography,* 4(2), 130–134.

3

Death: 'It's Sexy and Stuff'

Introduction

This chapter is the first of three to promote the views of young participants in this study to the forefront of end-of-life discussions. In particular, it explores the young-people's observations and reflections on portrayals of death across a variety of media sources. The chapter utilises some data and discussions previously presented in the journal *Mortality: Promoting the interdisciplinary study of death and dying* under the title 'Death wears a T-shirt—Listening to young people talk about death' (Coombs 2014: 284–302). However, more extensive and wide-ranging conversations are presented here and the debates, arguments and discussions surrounding them are further elaborated, developed and extended.

Death, it would appear, is certainly not a new concept for these young-people but rather a highly visible part of their everyday lives. Films, books, the internet and news media all peddle mortality vociferously, providing an easily accessible platform for readily available death related images and discussions. Replete with the 'glamour' of celebrity deaths and enticingly attractive vampires, exploding superheroes and woolly mammoths, these conversations combine the highly

© The Author(s) 2017
S. Coombs, *Young People's Perspectives on End-of-Life*,
Studies in Childhood and Youth, DOI 10.1007/978-3-319-53631-6_3

extraordinary with more mundane and everyday aspects of life and death. It might be considered that such forms allow death to be considered at a safe distance, not too close and not too tangible. However, this potentially 'safe space' is eagerly entered and investigated, leaving death, culture and youth to collide in an array of colourful resources and reflections on the strange and the commonplace.

The Stuff of Nightmares (2007) is a young-adult fiction novel written by Malory Blackman. The book personifies death as a teenage girl who wears black jeans and a T-shirt, on which is inscribed '**I am you dearest wish, I am your worst nightmare**'. Megan (aged 15), and one of the participants in the study, reads and shares this description further, quoting a paragraph from the book to illustrate the impression it has on her thoughts about death; something to be feared, never predictable but above all as romantic. The book provides Megan with a source or resource from which her ideas, in relation to death and dying, are drawn. Within the source is a story, which was read, enjoyed, interpreted and challenged. Embedded within the story are multiple 'cultural scripts' relating to depictions of death in various forms. This book therefore, represents an everyday material object that spoke to Megan of death and from which she could examine and expand her outlook on issues of mortality. The following chapter adopts this framework by examining ways in which commonly available sources, stories and scripts are used, challenged and incorporated into young-people's death-related thinking.

It is important to contextualise, *sources, stories, scripts and stuff,* further. Images and discourses in relation to death are available from many sources; television, literature, cinema, newspaper and the internet, and in the words of Hallam and Hockey, they can 'evoke the dead' (2001: 2). Children in contemporary Western societies have ready access to these and the information they provide; in fact, it is possible to contend that they lead media saturated lives (Livingstone 2009). Media sources, report countless stories of death, many of which emanate from broad themes; natural disasters, violent, unexpected and war related deaths. These overarching types are linked to specific stories: for example, the death of a celebrity such as Jade Goody, particular groups raising money for a dying child to go on a holiday to Disneyland, the efforts of individuals to stop leaking radiation from a stricken nuclear power plant in Japan or fictional stories. The stories, in turn, contain a variety of cultural scripts relating to dominant discourses within the narrative, which point to death as variously heroic, romantic, tragic, expected or unexpected, good or bad. Seale suggests that a huge variety of 'cultural representations' of death are available and refers to them as 'discourses on death' or 'cultural scripts' that can be incorporated into individuals 'biographical situations' (1998: 4). Each story may have one or many death-related scripts attached to it.

Young-people are clearly able to access death related information through media sources, stories and scripts. However, as the following chapters will demonstrate, they are not just passive receivers of the information but active in constructing their own responses. The previous chapter highlighted the use of household objects to uncover young-people's understanding of death. Interestingly, Prout notes that mundane objects are 'a very important part of the everyday worlds of children' (2005: 116) and have recently been used to explore their participation in social life and powers of agency. Consequently, using household 'stuff' enabled these young-people to travel back-and-forth across the topic of death, drawing upon the sources, stories and scripts available to them, and in so doing tell their own end-of-life stories.

Armstrong-Coster in her study of cancer related pathographies suggests that 'life in present day Western society is significantly influenced by the media' and therefore, 'it is perhaps not surprising that this is where individuals turn to for knowledge' (2005: 110). Arguments relating to media influences on children are plentiful. Buckingham (2011) indicates that children today engage with the media more than any other activity and that the ideas, images, and representations available to them, inevitably shape their views. Considerable media content explicitly relates to death and dying and thus death becomes a highly visible entity in young-people's lives. This chapter uncovers ways in which the young utilise death-related media content, whilst at the same time indicating an awareness of its unrealistic nature, and therefore its far cry from the actuality of death and dying.

Howarth positions the media as a significant 'marker of popular culture and social mores surrounding death and dying' (2007: 21).

Certainly these young-people's accounts reflect this, alongside of Earle and Komaromy's observations that 'death and dying are richly represented in poetry, fiction and the media' and that narratives range from the deeply personal to 'others that provide structure and order to the way death and dying can be understood' (2009: 25). Weinstein directs us to 'opening ourselves up to understanding loss [via] the use of poetry, prose and film' (2002: 197), and points to different genres as poignant and powerful ways to introduce and share knowledge and understanding. He continues by suggesting that depictions of death, dying and loss, written outside of the academic sphere, provide valuable insights into a range of experiences and emotions.

Conversations presented in this chapter demonstrate how the medias continuous source of narratives and 'cultural scripts' are adopted and/ or adapted into the 'lifeworld' (Howarth 2007: 103) of these young-people. Knox argues, that in relation to contemporary *ars moriendi* resources such as film provide 'social scripts for dying' (2006: 234). Berridge concurs, stating that in visually led cultures 'the lens, the camera, the screen is integral to our exposure to representations of death' (2002: 247). Our fear of death, Berridge continues, is 'chiefly performance anxiety about dying' (2002: 7) and therefore, the only cure for this is 'rehearsal' (Knox 2006: 234). Arguably then, the films young-people watch, the books they read, the television programmes they view, provide opportunities to rehearse reactions and responses to death and to explore their own and other people's mortality.

Ellie (aged 15) notes how media representations affect her thoughts and reactions to death.

> I think they [the media] influence your perceptions and understanding of death and what happens after death and the way you should behave. In films it's often very melodramatic, there's lots of screaming and crying, but it doesn't show that people cope with death in many different ways. Some people just go really silent.

This account highlights Ellie's agreement with notions of media influence and yet she challenges some of these portrayals as unrealistic. In calling to mind the filmic images portrayed, she questions the representation of 'screaming and crying' as a response to death and considers the possibility of a variety of other reactions, including silence. The sections that follow emphasise this approach; illustrating first the participants' involvement with a particular media representation, followed by challenges to it, and leaving the final and often poignant inference to them. The following conversations highlight these young-peoples' acceptance of, testing and objections to, prevailing cultural scripts, beginning with romanticism.

You Find Yourself Falling in Love with Vampires

Sontag (1978) powerfully argues that the disease tuberculosis (TB) has been represented in romantic, passionate and even erotic ways, throughout literature. The result has been a portrayal of pale, young and beautiful men and women facing their unavoidable yet idealistic and ultimately redemptive deaths. She maintains that the romantic treatment of death ensures 'that people were made singular, made more interesting, by their illness' (1978: 31), and that this 'goes with the inveterate spiritualising of TB and the sentimentalizing of its horrors' (1978: 41). Sontag's observations strike-a-cord with an amount of romanticised and possibly mawkish portrayals of death from within a variety of contemporary media and literary sources, these are clearly identified in the following conversations.

One example, keenly and enthusiastically embraced, was depicted in the popular books and films of the *Twilight.* series; vampire-themed romance novels by American author Stephanie Meyer. Death here, as noted by Jo (aged 15), is present in the shape of a young male vampire who is beautiful, pallid, erotic and romantic in equal measure. A romantic script is clearly present within the novels, situated within the love and enduring/never-ending romance of the two central characters. The sources, that is books and films in this case, encouraged reflection on the links between love, death and romance but equally inspired the young-people to challenge these and confront their own constructions of what death and dying really meant to them.

Jo: *Twilight* is all about love and death, and that love conquers everything, even death. It's about Bella and Edward. Edward is a vampire and therefore he's dead already [pause]. In the third book, I think it's the third, maybe the fourth, Bella nearly dies giving birth to their baby and she has to drink Edward's blood to survive and then she becomes a vampire. Edward wasn't always a vampire, he was saved from a normal death by his stepfather, when he was a boy. Edward, in the films, is played by Robert Pattinson and most girls think he's gorgeous, I don't, but in the books he's described as very beautiful. He's pale, with skin that sparkles in the sun and he has orange eyes. It's basically a love story because at the end Edward and Bella live together forever, well 'live' might be the wrong word, they are 'undead' together forever.

Initially, Jo's account reflects a romantic cultural script, centred on notions of beauty, love, youth and adversity, and the frequently expressed belief that love conquers everything, even death. However, whilst engaging in the romantic script, the love story, Jo expresses the view that death, in this case, is different, as the main character is a vampire and therefore dead already. Thus Jo views, the representation of death throughout the twilight series as 'out of the ordinary'. She develops this idea further, explaining that in order to be 'saved from a normal death', the two main characters, Bella and Edward, must become vampires, the 'undead', then they can be together forever. This romantic script is reminiscent of classic narratives such as Romeo and Juliet, where in order to share eternity the key players must die. Teenage vampire fiction, currently popular with young-people in contemporary Western society, is arguably a symptom of increasing secularisation, where traditional beliefs associated with an afterlife are being questioned. Therefore, Bella and Edward must enter a different reality in order for their intimacy to flourish. The theme of the undead, often explored within this type of literature and therefore a deviation from the normality of death, is commented on further by Amy (aged 15).

Amy: I mean there are books like the *Twilight* series which are about vampires but they are about the undead, so nobody really dies in those. So death is something different in those.

There is a clear acknowledgement from both Amy and Jo that death in these books and films is 'different', thereby reaffirming that 'real' deaths are unlikely to be so romantic. However, the passionate involvement of the two central vampire characters draws the young-people into the narrative and enables them to think about death from an alternative perspective, that of the undead. Young-people then, either accept, discard or engage in further contemplation on this concept. Howarth (2007) notes that the trope of the undead remains popular in contemporary media. Within it the demarcation between the living and the dead is seen as 'fragile' and the boundaries of mortality less clear, a greater emphasis now being placed on 'the dead and the undead come[ing] to live amongst us' (2007: 106). Jo reflects the view that the undead are more prominent in society today, and that through sources such as the *Twilight* series, they, as young-people, are increasingly able to discuss a variety of different approaches to death and dying.

> Jo: I think we're all getting a lot more used to death though, because we're all watching films and reading books about vampires and the undead and that sort of thing. You find yourself talking about them as though they were alive, and falling in love with vampires, and therefore like dead people. [All laugh]. So it's really like obscure but people are getting more used to death because of the *Twilight*, *House of Night*, sort of thing.

Interestingly, I mentioned the 'vampire' stories to a group of similar aged boys who gave very different accounts of these fictional narratives. The focus here, in contrast to the girls' emphasis on aesthetics and enduring love, was much less concerned with romance and more by the sexual relationships inherent within the novels and films.

> SC   :I've spoken to a lot of girls who are really into these 'vampire' films. How do you feel about them?
>
> All: [Emphatic shaking of heads, mutters of 'yuck' and 'no'. Then pointing at Chris and laughing]
>
> Chris: (aged 14): Yeah well, I don't mind them, *Twilight* and *True Blood* and stuff.

Ted (aged 15): It's like watching a porn film. [All laugh]

Syed (aged 15): How would you know Ted? [All laugh...Ted now quite embarrassed]

SC : What do you mean Ted?

Ted : Well it's just a bit risqué. Ok, it's sexy and stuff. [All laugh]. Ok [pause]. Well moving on [he laughs]. I've been thinking about werewolves all day. [All laugh]

The boys initially denied any interest in these films at all, suggesting quite disparagingly that they were for girls. However, despite their professed disinterest in the romantic elements of the script, they were more willing to discuss the sexual content. Ted, in a somewhat embarrassed way, raised the complex relationship between sex, death and pornography by suggesting that these vampire films were like watching a pornographic movie, 'sexy' in some way. The elements of the romantic script, identified by Sontag (1978) as erotic, were more prominent in the boy's discussions. Ted did not explicitly say why he thought the films were sexy, perhaps inhibited by the context in which he suddenly found himself centre stage, but nevertheless a link was implied. Death and sex have often been seen as taboo subjects. Gorer (1955) suggested that death had replaced sex as a source of pornographic entertainment. However, Bronfen (1992) in her discussion of Stoker's *Dracula*, positions the vampire as a motif for western attitudes towards death. She argues that this frequently used trope, demonstrates human uncertainties in relation to sexual desire and fear of mortality, 'with the theme of sexuality put forward to veil that of death' (1992: 313).

Perhaps then, it is possible to suggest that the popularity of teenage vampire fiction, referred to by Jo (aged 15) in an earlier discussion as 'vampire porn', may promote the sexual and romantic elements in order to 'veil' the central underlying theme of death. However, these young-people discussed romance, sex and death equally and without hesitation, although some gender differences were apparent.

It is interesting at this point to note Postman's argument, in which he blames the media for the disappearance of childhood and furthermore, that the opening up of topics, such as death, to children 'poses dangers and makes the future of childhood problematic' (1982: 87). However, these conversations seem to suggest that vampire narratives, such as the ones discussed above, are part of youth culture, that young-people actively consume these stories, and far from destroying child-hood they allow the staging and exploration of a variety of unusual and similarly, more commonplace approaches to death. Postman's thinking, Prout contends, 'tends to be suffused with nostalgic longing for child-hood to remain the same' (2005: 15), whereas childhood, like all aspects of social life and death is, as previously discussed, continually changing. As the barriers between adult and child become less clearly defined, so they do between life and death and these young-people demonstrate an awareness of it throughout these conversations. Therefore, I argue that gaining knowledge about death from a variety of media sources cannot be blamed for the disappearance of childhood but rather the appearance of a childhood in which death, in all its different and eclectic guises, is less invisible. This diversity of representations should not give adults cause for concern but rather encourage death as a meaningful and wide-ranging topic, worthy of exploration, rather than being whispered about in hushed tones.

Similar connections with the romantic elements of death, previously uncovered in the *Twilight* series, were also found in Megan's descrip-tion of the following book. Here death is depicted as a teenage girl who accompanies a boy in and out of his classmates' personal nightmares [previously discussed at the start of this chapter]. Again the presentation of love as denied in life but undeniable in death persists. Megan does not question the romantic script, as has been the case in previous dis-cussions, but accepts it as beautiful and as a sense of relief that death no longer poses a danger to the couple in this story.

> **Megan** (aged 15): This [she holds up *The Stuff of Nightmares*] is a book with lots of death in it. It's really scary, it's got lots of death in it.
>
> **Charlotte** (aged 15): It gave me nightmares.
>
> **Megan:** It's about this guy who goes on a school trip and they all have a train crash and he finds out that he can go into the nightmares of his classmates and his teacher. Yes, and on the train is this girl in a T-shirt

that says 'I am your dearest wish, I am your worst nightmare' and it turns out she's death, and goes in and out of the nightmares with him. In all the really bad nightmares she is there and awful things happen and it's really scary. I think in one of the nightmares she's not there but then the people in that one are already dead. In some of the others someone gets turned to stone, someone kills their grandchildren and themselves [hesitates]. The best one is where a girl gets killed because she fell in love with the wrong man, and because they are from different classes they get buried in different cemeteries but they get back together as ghosts. They walk past the fence and out of the cemetery together but they can hear all the other dead people shouting at them. It's really scary but beautiful and death can't get them anymore.

Despite Megan's unquestioning acceptance of the romantic script she juggles conflicting ideas and representations of death. The traditional image of the grim reaper, complete with hood and scythe is gone, replaced by a teenage girl in a T-shirt. This figure elicits a fearful reaction from Megan, despite or because of the fact that death in this guise, appears similar to herself. Conversely, death is also the bringer of possibilities, as life and death, fear and freedom, the world of the living and the spirit world all exist together in Megan's seemingly simple but indeed highly complex account. Traditional and contemporary views of death appearing side-by-side. Theories that construct society as 'death denying' are founded on universal fears of death (Becker 1973); everyone's worst nightmare. Paradoxically, this account alludes to the possibility that death might also be 'everyone's dearest wish', a possible source of new horizons, not just the traditional heavens but other spaces too. Megan demonstrates how young-people have the capacity to integrate traditional and contemporary ideas of death, creating individual responses and 'opening up terrain eschewed by those who see such a topic as either depressing or pointless' (Hockey et al. 2010: 233).

The book, as described by Megan, continues the theme of love triumphing over death and the possibility of 'life' discrete from death. Howarth (2007) suggests that in pre-modern societies death was seen as a certainty but not necessarily as the end, as beliefs in an afterlife were strong. Conversely, that in postmodern societies thoughts and interests relating to an afterlife have changed, largely influenced by altered patterns of mortality, challenges to the dominance of medicine and science, and a decline in the established church. Thus leading to 'a range of beliefs that challenge separation' (Howarth 2007: 258). I suggest therefore, that the changing approaches to death noted above, and to childhood as discussed previously, acknowledge the diversity of childhoods and the constantly changing approaches to death that young-people, like Megan, are able to access and incorporate into their thoughts on mortality.

Another group of teenagers, discussed various films and DVDs they had watched, for example *My Sister's Keeper*, *The Time Traveller's Wife*, and *Seven Pounds*, all of which detailed further romantic representations of death and highlighted the girls' responses to them. McInerney argues that such films are often categorised as either the 'weepie genre' (2009: 228) or as 'women's films' (2009: 211), and often portray death in the context of passive acceptance akin to sacrifice, or an 'opportunity for growth' (2009: 228). The deaths described are largely unconventional, bearing little resemblance to reality but occupying a softer more 'feminized' (2009: 212) approach to dying. The main characters are often described in some depth so that their demise, when it comes, is more meaningful and more emotional to the viewer. The sentimentalising of death in this way can ignore and distance the actuality of the event, whilst allowing the viewer to be caught up in the emotionality. Here Amy and then Laura (both aged 15) describe those feelings.

> **Amy:** I watched *The Time Traveller's Wife* and at the end of that the guy dies and I cried for hours after that. I wasn't just sitting in the cinema with tears streaming down [she touches her face with her two index fingers and draws the false tears on herself]. I was actually like sobbing. People were like laughing at me and my friends wouldn't talk to me because I was embarrassing them because I was sobbing so much, and I couldn't even stop crying when we got to MacDonald's.

This indicates Amy's emotional involvement and response to the film and of those around her. The actual death of the main character is hardly mentioned ... 'the guy dies'. Laura recounts a similar story and her response.

Laura: This has Will Smith in. [She holds up the DVD: *Seven Pounds*]

Jack (aged 16): Oh I've seen that.

Laura: It's really, really sad. Shall I tell you all about it?

SC: Yes

Laura: Well, this guy accidentally kills seven people in a car crash, and he feels really bad about it and that he's a murderer and stuff. So he decides he's going to transform seven people's lives to make up for it. So he gives this woman his house, and this other woman needed a heart transplant and he fell in love with her, so he killed himself to give his heart to the woman he loved, and I cried for about half an hour after I'd seen it. I just love it.

The transforming nature of death is an obvious cultural script within these romantic narratives, clearly picked out by the girls and one with which they identify. Not only are the central characters the bringers of death but also saviours, as they sacrifice their lives for others. The woman, whose life continues due to the sacrifice of others, appears to have little say in the matter and is a passive recipient of the ultimate gift of life.

Finally, Laura discusses a different film, *My Sister's Keeper*.

Laura: Well I've got one more thing and that's a film ticket to see *My Sister's Keeper*. Because it's basically about controlling other people's lives and having the chance to find out if you can save someone else's life or whatever. Amy can probably explain it because she read the book.

Amy: The book is very different from the film so shall I explain the book.

Laura: Yes

Amy: In the book, it isn't the girl with leukaemia who dies it's her sister, and her kidney is donated to her sister with leukaemia. So that messed me up really [pause], because all the way through the book I was expecting the girl with leukaemia to die, and 'boof' her sister dies, and I was like, well that wasn't supposed to happen. And then I was like, well, perhaps death is like that and you don't know when it's going to come and you can't prepare for it so you need to be ready for it whenever. But if you spent your whole time worrying about it you wouldn't really be living so you need to be aware of it, but not dwell on it all the time.

Laura: To me it like brings in ideas about 'letting die'. If someone has a serious illness like leukaemia and if people are in a lot of pain and they want to die, then they should be allowed to choose.

Jack: The individual needs to make their own choice, cos like some people can't speak or can't communicate very well, it doesn't mean they want to die. It might be that the family sees them suffering and thinks they want to die and that they as relatives know what is best, but it's not necessarily the right thing to do. It's difficult to know who's in control then.

This account, whilst initially fitting well with a romantic script that covers the love of two sisters, the sacrifice of one for the other, the aesthetic beauty of the two leading roles and the tragedy of young and unexpected death, was in fact the conduit for some challenging discussions. Amy, for example, was shocked by the unexpected death of one of the sisters and the message she took from this was that death was often like this in reality, uncertain and untimely. Laura, comments that the film made her think about 'letting die', that perhaps we sometimes try to preserve life at all costs and that in some situations people should decide if they want to live or die. Jack encourages caution when discussing choices made at the end-of-life, as he feels that this must be an individual's choice but that other powerful influences might have more control over death than the person themselves. As can be discerned within these conversations young-people are not 'cultural dopes' and readily distinguish fantasy from reality within filmic and other portrayals of death and dying

The portrayal of dying within the framework of romantic scripts is popular. McInerney points to a significant amount of films that present dying in a romantic light, 'depicting a soft-focused and wistful dying—a true 'fade to black' (2009: 211). Howarth notes that whilst death is present in a great many films 'it is distanced from the audience and bears little resemblance to the everyday experience of dying' (2007: 104). Young-people drew upon these romantic cultural images and used them to enter into discussions about death and dying. Many of the sources they brought, whilst ostensibly opening up the subject of death, could been seen to distance them from the reality of natural deaths. However, this did not seem to be the case as they continually questioned these romantic representations.

Finally, within the context of romantic cultural scripts I would like to highlight Charlotte's story of her father's illness, which portrays, for her, the reality of potential death. Whilst romance and the representations of it were highly popular areas for discussion, the reality of life and death often cut across these conversations, providing space for the sharing of directly personal experience. I would like Charlotte's words to stand alone, as a powerful story that demonstrates her ability to reject the romantic script and adult held assumptions that young-people do not, cannot and should not think about death. Charlotte's narrative falls far short of the romance and rhetoric portrayed in literature, art and film. In contrast, the stark reality of her lived experience situates death as neither romantic, aesthetically pleasing or sentimental. Charlotte clearly demonstrates her understanding that fantasy is not reality, and that death in this determining moment, does not wear a T-Shirt but rather makes her feel physically 'sick'. The source, the story and the script, are therefore all hers.

> **Charlotte** (aged 15): Well some of the things that are in our boxes are just things, but these are real experiences [pause]. Going back to what Ellie said about not wanting to remember her Grandma in a certain way just before she died. My Dad, just at the end of the summer holidays last year, got appendicitis and so he went to hospital and they nicked a vein or something, and he came really close to dying but I hadn't been told that, so then they said something's gone a little bit wrong, he'll be fine, he'll be fine. I think I'd have gone really off the rails if he had died because I wasn't told he was so ill. When we went to see him in hospital he looked really ill, he looked green, and really, really thin and I had to go to the toilet because I felt I was going to be sick, but it wasn't because I don't love him it's because it's so different from how you normally see them, usually happy and healthy and throwing a tennis ball around. He couldn't laugh, he couldn't smile, he was really ill and I didn't want to remember him like that, so I sort of blocked it all out, but it didn't help at all really.

I Want to Die like Peter Petrelli

Arguments surrounding the presence or absence of death in the media continue apace. Walter (2008a, b, 2009), as highlighted previously, argues that the presence of death in society is increasing, particularly within the mass media. Seale suggests that this 'open awareness' of death is 'particularly suited to the conditions of late modernity' (1995: 610), and Hanusch acknowledges that the news media is replete with 'reports about death and destruction' (2010: 1). It is within such media stories that heroic accounts of death come to the fore. These highly poignant depictions of death often relate to war and remembrance, and attempt to imbue such dying with meaning. Their representation is abundant, arguably due to recent, high profile wars in Iraq, Afghanistan and the Middle East. Seale refers to different forms of heroism, 'ordinary heroism' (1998: 56), 'traditional masculine heroism' (1995: 611) or a 'specifically female heroic' (1995: 599) that contains an explicit care and concern for others. He goes on to compare these with everyday life, suggesting that everyday life is 'routine, repetitive and mundane', whereas the heroic is imbued with 'self-defining moments … of courage and sacrifice' (1995: 599).

Deaths containing these heroic elements, from the everyday hero to the superhero were evident in these conversations. Discussions centred around the vibrant, dramatic and epic deaths of superheroes, the courageous and self-sacrificing deaths of soldiers, and the brave actions of 'everyday' heroes. Dominant cultural scripts contextualised death as variably inspirational, noble and sacrificial. As we shall see, these highly active representations of death, so popular within the superhero genre, were selected by the young-people as something to aspire to.

Sally (aged 15) began the exploration of heroic scripts by discussing the notion of 'heroism' in Louisa May Alcott's novel *Little Women*.

> **Sally:** Well I've got *Little Women* because I read this when I was about 9, and both brothers go to war and the older one Charlie goes first, and is shot for being a coward.
>
> **Charlotte** (aged 15): He wasn't a coward though, was he?

Sally: No he wasn't, but like it's really significant to me, it made me think. I don't know why, but I just thought that was a horrible way to die. Like you go to war to fight for the country you believe in, and then get shot by the people who sent you and who your comrades were and ... [pause, shakes her head].

Charlotte: But he was shot for staying with his injured brother wasn't he?

Sally: Yes, he stayed with his brother, and they shot him for being a coward and not fighting on the front line like everyone else. So even though he was being helpful and being a hero in his own way he wasn't being a hero in the way they wanted him to be.

Sally identifies two heroic deeds here. The first acknowledges a young man prepared to die for his country, thereby reflecting Seale's view of traditional masculine heroism. The second recognises his actual death, being shot as a coward, for staying with his injured brother rather than returning to the front line. Sally asserts that this is unjust, as she identifies the action of staying with his brother as equally heroic, reflecting her concern for the more meaningful and personal relationship between himself and his brother, a more female heroic perhaps, involving 'emotional expression and self-sacrifice' (Seale 1995: 599). Here, Sally juggles two depictions of heroic scripts and expresses her moral verdict. Mayall contends that children and young-people's moral judgement is often sequestered, encouraging the view 'that [children] do not engage in socially useful activities and hence their moral agency is downgraded' (2002: 111). Sally however, clearly shows her competence in discussing morally ambiguous questions. Her exploration of heroic death incorporates different dying scripts and indicates her engagement with highly complex social representations of death and dying. She deftly concludes that heroism is defined in different ways by different people and within different contexts.

Sally and Charlotte continue their exploration of heroic death through a further extract from *Little Women*.

Sally: I've just realised she doesn't die in this book but at the very beginning of the next book, but... [pause].

Charlotte: She dies in the film

Megan (aged 15): Who does?

Charlotte: Oh Megan haven't you read the book? Beth dies.

Sally and Charlotte together: She gets scarlet fever.

Sally: And it was like a terminal illness then, but she recovers and everyone's really happy, and in the midst of everyone being really happy about Meg getting married and having the baby, and Amy and Lorrie getting together then they forget about the fact that Beth is really weak. I mean they don't literally forget about her, but they forget she is getting weaker and weaker.

Charlotte: She tries to protect everybody from the fact she's dying

Sally: Yes, she tries to protect everyone. In the film she says she's not scared, she wants to go. She says you're all good at things and I've got nothing to live for. There's nothing I'm really good at and nothing to live for, nothing I'm amazingly good at. It's very sad… [pause]… but brave.

Both Charlotte and Sally see this act as both poignant and 'brave'; Beth protects her family from the reality of her death by reconciling them to it through her own fearless acceptance, and thereby makes it easier for those who participate in her death and live on after it. Acknowledgement of death, discussed previously as a form of 'open awareness', is a script often used to signify heroism and bravery and indicates that death might be desirable in some way. Sally and Charlotte note these themes and find Beth's final evaluation that everyone else had something to live for, and therefore her death is less significant, as a heroic act and a gift to her family.

These two examples, introduced initially by Sally, contain elements of self-sacrifice and a willingness to give up one's own life for others. They equally highlight differences between male and female heroism, so often depicted in the media. McInerney argues that 'violent, agonal moments occupy what might be called the "harder", more masculine end of this spectrum, with "softer" dying inhabiting the more "feminized" end' (2009: 212). Sally's choice of heroic deaths fit these frameworks. Charlie's death is sudden, violent, and situated away from friends and family, while Beth's deathbed scene is much softer, situated within the domestic sphere, surrounded by the people she loves and centred around a gradual but valiant and courageous fading away. Sally is keen to emphasise that heroism takes many forms, and stress her admiration for the protagonists and the contrasting ways in which they die. Becker's discussion of heroic death seems pertinent at this point as he imagines that,

> We admire most the courage to face death; we give such valour our highest and most constant adoration; it moves us deeply in our hearts because we have doubts about how brave we ourselves would be. When we see a man bravely facing his own extinction we rehearse the greatest victory we can imagine. And so the hero has been the centre of human honour and acclaim since probably the beginning of specifically human evolution (1973: 11).

Heroic scripts of death are not only apparent in literature but are vibrantly depicted through television drama. The death of superhero character Peter Petrelli, in the TV series *Heroes*, captures the young-people's attention.

Laura (aged 15): I'd like to die exploding in the air to save the world like Peter Petrelli. [All laugh]

Amy (aged 15): Oh dear!

Laura: I love him! [All laugh]

SC: So do programmes like that influence your ideas about death in any way?

Amy: I think I feel a connection there, as sort of aspiration that I would rather die like that. I mean I'd rather go out with a bang [emphasises the word] than be boring and go to sleep.

Laura: And also, Claire [reference to another character in the programme] she can't be hurt, that's her super power, so she's never going to die, and things like superheroes are they ever going to die? [Short silence and then laughing}

SC: I don't know the answer to that.

Jack (aged 16): I don't think that what might happen to a bunch of superheroes is going to influence my ideas of death because they are nothing close to the truth, cos they have flying people and things like that.

Laura: Yeah, yeah, I know, I think that too, but he is a hero.

This way of dying appears to hold an attraction, despite the ready acknowledgment that superhero deaths of this type are fantastical and extreme. This was no lingering death, no protracted suffering leading to dust and decay, instead death is 'action packed, high octane, superhuman and of epic proportions' (Coombs 2014: 293). Amy suggests that such deaths are inspirational, even aspirational and she would rather die in this explosive, vibrant and purposeful way than, as Seale describes, 'a slow decline without reaching a dramatic moment of dying' (1995: 609). In this way the young-people select a more dramatic script as preferable for themselves, and despite Jack and Laura's questioning of the value and 'truth' of such fantasy images, Laura reinforces her preference for life to end with a bang rather than a whimper, whilst conceding that this is unlikely.

Further exploration of heroic scripts demonstrates the connection between war and remembrance and the heroic act of saving others. Berridge argues that the twentieth century was the age of 'mass death and the mass media' (2002: 62) and that we are now 'oblivious' to the amount of information and images set before us. However commonplace media reporting on death has become these young-people are certainly not oblivious to it. A variety of heroic themes were considered, many associated with the World Wars, in which 'dying with dignity' (Berridge 2002: 23) was presented as a dominant heroic script. Equally present, are the more recently viewed repatriation of bodies, of service men and women from wars in Afghanistan and Iraq. Hanusch (2010) argues that due to a number of governments' concerns about public reactions to graphic coverage of recent wars there are relatively few highly explicit images of death in the media. Potentially, I argue, this may account for the more sanitised versions of patriotism incorporated in the thinking, reactions and conversations of these young-people. Charlotte's choice of a You Tube clip perhaps illustrates this point.

Charlotte (aged 15): I've watched some videos on You Tube and there was this like man, he was a soldier, who came back from Afghanistan and came into his daughter's class and when she saw him she just sobbed and couldn't say anything. It gave me a lump in my throat even though I don't know them.

Charlotte's description is one that is geographically removed from the actuality of war, providing an image of the returning war hero, both father and soldier, made more poignant by the fact that he has 'escaped' death. This removes the viewer from the actual horrors of conflict, whilst maintaining a heroic but arguably sentimental icon of war. The soldier returns to his daughter within the context of school, a place of youth, innocence and life, a space that belongs to childhood, kept away from the corrupting influences of the adult world of war and death. The contrast between the child and the adult world is amplified through the dichotomies of the images; the strength of the father/soldier compared to the vulnerability of the child, and the heroic male figure versus the crying female child with whom Charlotte appears to identify. No words are spoken within this image, Charlotte's description is similar to viewing a painting. Her emotional response is created by the heroic imagery within the clip and influenced by cultural scripts situated within the discourses of both childhood and heroism. In this way Charlotte's individual views and responses to death are constructed, as Howarth suggests, through 'social and cultural norms and experience' (2007: 261).

Using a more collectivist viewpoint, both James and Lucy (both aged 15) explore heroic deaths in relation to national acts of remembrance. The cultural scripts available in media portrayals of these events, emphasise youthful, heroic self-sacrifice alongside public, community/national responses. James talks about the sights and sounds of the Remembrance Sunday service that he recently attended and reflects upon his response to this event.

James: In association with death I've brought with me a beret. It's my beret; it's not somebody's who's dead. It was for the Remembrance Day we've just had, like Remembrance Sunday. It makes me think of death, not deaths close to you but deaths of other people that you somehow still feel for, even if you've never heard of them. I thought that Remembrance Day was quite a significant example of deaths, you know young men dying for their country, and yeah...[Pause extending into a reflective silence]. Sorry. [Further silence].

SC: You seem to have something else there James that links to this. What is it?

James: Yes, well this is bugle music. This was played by someone in the band that I play in. Cos on Remembrance Sunday we did the marching and somebody played that, you know, 'The Last Post', which is a very prominent thing that probably reminds pretty much everyone in this country about death, and probably elsewhere. Yeah. [Silence]

James' involvement in, and his recounting of the Remembrance Sunday parade, highlights in his words, the heroism of 'young men dying for their country', a script he admires. The sights and sounds of marching, the playing of The Last Post, the names of people he does not know but still feels a connection with, all construct a powerful cultural script and an emotive response from this young man and those of us listening to him. The silences that dominate this short exchange provided a powerful background that echoed the traditional 2 min silence for the dead.

For Lucy, a similar but more contemporary construction of heroism and death lies in the repeated media coverage of the repatriation of soldiers' bodies through the village of Wootton Bassett in Wiltshire.

Lucy: Wootton Bassett is on the news a lot at the moment.

Jo (aged 15): What's Wootton Bassett?

Lucy: It's the village where the hearses drive through with the bodies of the soldiers who have died in Afghanistan. The people who live there have said that for every single coffin that goes through they'll stand outside and be silent. They've done it so many times now. They did it for the first one, so they can't stop because that would be ridiculous, and every soldier is important. So each time they stand outside in silence. A complete town at a standstill.

Heroic images and themes pervade Lucy's telling of this event. The actual death of the soldier is once again hidden from view and the ritual stands in his place. Lucy is drawn into the media portrayal of these images; she is a respectful observer of the funeral hearse, the rows of silent people, and the stillness and silence of the town. The image may relate to a particular time and place but incorporates a collective response to the dominant heroic script; Lucy is now part of that response. The role of the media in representing these acts often relates to the ritualisation of death (Seale 1998), and an invocation of collective memory (Hanusch 2010). Kitch and Hume state that the news media 'have become the primary forum for the conveyance and construction of public grief today' (2008: xiv).

The Everyday Hero

Having studied teenage responses to differing cultural scripts, from masculine/feminine versions of heroism to the vibrant and exultant deaths of superheroes and the ritualisation of returning war heroes, we now turn to depictions of the 'everyday hero', a person plucked from obscurity into the full glare of media attention. A variety of these inspirational stories abound in the media, ranging from young children saving the life of a parent by contacting the emergency services to the timely intervention of an adult in rescuing a child from choking. Such momentous events produce popular media scripts, which place 'ordinary' people dangerously close to death, only to be saved in timely fashion. It is this heroic saving from death, which becomes the focus of the younger children's discussions. Justine (aged 11), through the use of a toy plane, suggests that people die in plane crashes. However, the focus of the discussion moves away from the possibility of dying in such an accident to the heroic saving of life.

> **Justine:** I've bought a plane [brings out a toy plane] because I was thinking people could die in plane crashes.
>
> **Tom** (aged 10): Yes, because it's really rare to survive a plane crash. Sometimes lots of people die.
>
> **Milly** (aged 10): Well not really because there was that one where the man landed the plane on the water and everyone survived. They came

out and sat on the wings and were rescued. They said the pilot was a hero because he saved everyone.

Tom: Really!! Didn't the plane sink?

Milly: No, it was Ok.

Charlie (aged 10): Well, if like a plane did land on the water it would probably take it a while to sink because planes are made of aluminium and that's a very light metal, so it would take a while. So enough time for the people to be rescued. Also you might have to be careful because if it had propellers they might chop your head off.

All: [Talk at once] Yuck! That's gross! [Laughter].

The risk of such a catastrophic and fatal tragedy is clearly identified by Justine and her friends but it is the strong affirmation of life in the face of death that is recognised as the heroic deed. Both manmade and large-scale natural disasters frequently dominate media coverage and therefore their inherent connections with death have the potential to threaten our feelings of safety in the world, our 'ontological security' (Giddens 1991: 36). However, Milly reflects upon how this specific threat was mitigated by the bravery of the individual pilot, and the much peddled script of life being snatched from the jaws of death, appealed to these young-people. Charlie (aged 10), neatly and with a certain amount of aplomb brought this conversation to a close. He turned the script of heroism and life overcoming death around by suggesting that even if your life is spared in such an event, existence remains tenuous and uncertain, there are always other dangers lurking, and no sooner are you saved from one thing than your head could be chopped off by a propeller.

Portrayals of death containing heroic narratives are plentiful, emanating from a range of sources and stories. Through the use of their own individual and collective possessions, these young-people spoke openly and eloquently about the images and narratives available to them. Media images merged with their own distinctive ideas, and interactions with other members of the group developed, defined and challenged their thoughts. As Sally correctly identified in the first conversation, definitions of heroism are different for everyone, however it is clear that cultural classifications contain a number of persistent characterisations, such as self-sacrifice for a greater cause. Examining these conversations reveals how tales of heroism, some real and some fantasy, infiltrate young-peoples' everyday lives and support their reflections on death and ways to die. In particular, these heroic deaths are seen as something to aspire to.

Acts of heroism in the face of death are crucial cultural scripts, identified across a range of circumstances in Western societies, wars, disasters, accidents, to name a few, and this final extract is no exception. Presented here is the ultimate heroic battle, represented as child versus disease, and therefore by extension, innocence versus evil, good versus bad, sacred versus profane, indeed the threat to everything contemporary Western society holds dear about childhood. Dixon-Woods et al. suggest that newspaper accounts of childhood illness, in this case cancer, construct 'a threat to the entitlements and category bound activities of childhood', filling the pages with 'courageous, stoical and inspirational' (2003: 143) dying children. Similarly, Sontag (1978), in exploring how metaphors are used to describe illness, suggests that cancer is depicted as a battle, a fight against alien invasion, a war. Both evaluations, Sontag and Dixon-Woods, fit well with the concept of cultural scripts, providing a view of how death and dying is constructed, a lens through which death can be viewed.

The battle portrayed below is not purely the child's, it is the community's fight and is made more poignant by the unique circumstances of this particular mother and child. Justine (aged 11) bravely narrates the story. The script is clearly heroic, the scene is set for a final contest but Justine recognises and makes us aware that the child will die and the fight will be lost. This death is no Peter Petrelli, no returning hero, no self-sacrificing male or resigned female, no rehearsal for the greatest death we can imagine, this death will perhaps not sell papers, so the heroism will ultimately be forgotten. Once again the section ends with the words of one of the young-people and so Justine eloquently expresses the sorrow embedded in the potential loss of this child. She identifies the heroic determination of the community, the anguish of the mother and child, the tragedy of a short life, and finally acknowledges her own beliefs that no amount of money or effort can improve the outcome of this situation. Justine admires the heroic courage illustrated by the all the characters in this account but perhaps more poignantly and expressively exposes the desolation and finality of it.

> **Justine:** My dad, at work, had this charity day and one of the workers there is the mother of a child who has a really bad disease. I can't remember what the name of the disease was, but they are raising money for it so the little child doesn't die. Apparently the woman, it was quite hard for her to give birth or to get pregnant so she might not be able to have another baby. Her baby is two now, but she only has like two months left to live. She's only had a really short life and has had to fight to stay alive, which is very sad. She's had to fight and she's so little, and her Mum might not be able to have another baby. Everyone's trying to get lots of money to save her [short pause] but I don't think they will.

If They Stab You ... That's It!

UK newspaper headlines and TV reports increasingly contain startling headlines in relation to young-people and violent crime, in particular knife crime. For example, 'Knife crime every 24seconds' (Boden 2007), or 'One third of children admit to carrying a gun or knife' (Russell 2009). Such stories often generate prominent cultural scripts around risk and fear in the lives of young-people, and are clearly evident in these conversations. Perhaps, given the close age proximity of the participants to such high profile incidents and their clear identification with them at a local and neighbourhood level, it is not surprising that these discussions, in particular, were characterised by recognition and direct fear for their own lives, and became a major topic of discussion across all age groups.

A knife, in many shapes and forms, was the most common item brought along for discussion and indeed the object that most children said they wanted to include in their boxes. Knives were discussed in the context of killing, the gangs that might be carrying them and feelings of vulnerability as the possible targets of knife crime. The links to mortality, whilst not always stated, were often present. Fear of possible death arose more readily in these discussions than elsewhere, perhaps due to the ever-present cultural links between knife crime and youth. Howarth (2007) points to the medias important role in raising awareness of this type of risk and also in posing it as a major threat to life. Whilst this may be so, Seale argues that 'media representations are not simply absorbed by readers and viewers' (1998: 123). Certainly this was case in some of the following conversations, where in opposition to dominant scripts of violence and loss of life, the knife was redefined in terms of creativity.

Some of the younger children discuss their fears of knife crime.

Milly (aged 10): Yes, but I did want to bring my brother's penknife but he wouldn't let me, because I thought people do get killed by knives and guns sometimes, you see it on the news and in the papers.

SC: Does that worry you?

Milly: Well [pause]. Sort of [pause]. It doesn't really worry me [pause]. Not that much [pause].

Lottie (aged 10): It worries me in places like London.

Tom (aged 10): It worries me sometimes, because of when we go out cycling. We have this alley near our house and I've seen lots of chavs hanging around there and if I'm on my own that worries me.

Milly: If I'm going out in the evening or something I go with [mentions brother's name], because there are lots of gangs that hang around out there, and I don't want to be on my own.

Charlie aged 10): It scares me because in the evening we have a house near us where lots of gangs hang out [pause].

Justine (aged 11): Yes, it's like a community house and like when you look out of the window they like look at you and shout at you and it's a bit worrying [pause].

Charlie: And annoying. I don't think they're going to kill me [pause], but I don't like it. I'm not sure what they will do.

Milly clearly indicates her concerns about knives and guns and states that her knowledge is gained from accounts in the media. Personal experience is clearly not required to enter into this discourse of fear, the cultural script is manifest and the young-people draw upon it for information. Milly begins by tentatively suggesting that she is not too concerned about the issue of knife crime but as the conversation progresses and moves closer to home she becomes more fearful. Lottie indicates that she would be afraid of knife crime in London. Whereas Tom associates knife crime with reference to 'chavs' and his insecurity at being isolated in an alley close to his home. Milly now also refers to 'gangs', her knowledge of the local spaces they inhabit and her fear of being alone in such places, to alleviate her concern she suggests always taking her brother with her. Charlie and Justine also refer to gangs and a space they occupy close to their home. The so-called gangs/chavs, in reality other children, are seen as threatening, scary, worrying and equally the spaces they occupy as potentially dangerous. James et al. suggest that 'children are particularly noticeable in relation to their setting' (1998: 37), that is they either occupy designated spaces such as school or are clearly in the wrong place and therefore up to no good. The cultural script relating to knife crime appears to be taken up by the young-people, who connect the spaces occupied by different groups designated as 'other than them' with their feelings of safety. Charlie suggests that although he does not think these people will kill him he is unsure of what they will do and he is clearly unhappy with the possibilities. Within this exchange, connections between the media and dominant scripts relating to knife crime are clearly evident. The highlighting, by the media, of young-people in the wrong place at the wrong time, as both killer and victim, leaves these young participants unambiguously fearful.

Moving to an older group, John (aged 15) brought two very different knives to the focus group; his Great Grandfather's knife that was used in World War II, and his Grandfather's knife that he describes as recreational. He contrasts these with the 'street knives' of today.

John: I brought my Great Granddad's knife [brings out huge knife], it was used in the war, the Second World War and I thought it was appropriate. I thought if I was bringing his ashes I might as well bring his knife. It was used in battle so I thought that was quite good. [One of the boys reaches out to touch the knife]. I wouldn't do that if I were you, it probably had blood on it.

Syed (aged 15): Cool! It's probably got pizza on it now [refers to refreshments provided]. [All laugh]

John: This is a Bowie knife [touches the blade of the knife very carefully, turns it around, gazes at it, puts it down. Brings out another knife]. This knife [shows it to everyone], it's all old and rusty and was my other Granddad's and it's got his initials on it, and I thought I wouldn't like that in me either. But this knife [he points to the first one] is about war, and this one [he holds up the knife] is about recreation. They're not like the knives you see on the streets today. They are just pointless. They are like for 'self-defence' that's not even needed. They wouldn't need to defend themselves or even start the stuff if other people didn't do it. So if we all didn't do it then there wouldn't be a problem, would there?

SC: Does it worry you?

All: Yes. Yeah. Definitely.

Syed: It's like you sometimes don't want to go out at night time, cos you never know if they are carrying a knife with them because if they stab you [pause]. That's it!

Chris (aged 14): I know someone who was stabbed in the leg. He was walking through [names place] park, it wasn't dark or anything, and a load of like chavs just ran out of the bushes and stabbed him in the leg. It was like for no reason at all. He was just like minding his own business.

John incorporates cultural scripts of heroism into the story of his Great Grandfather's bravery and contrasts this with the 'pointless' street knives used today. Syed and Chris, in a similar way to the younger participants, expressed their fear of being alone, of gangs and the violence associated with them. In contrast however, in the conversations of this older group, death is made more explicit. Chris talks from personal experience and his account includes traditional violent scripts of the lone innocent victim, violent out of control youths, public space, and an indiscriminate brutal attack. Such aggressive representations are unmistakably present in the news media.

A diverse range of death related ideas were explored through the object of the knife and the cultural scripts attached to it. The young-people compared and contrasted these; the knife as an instrument of heroism, of self-defence, of brutality, of fear, of injury and ultimately of death. A gradual verbalisation of finality. The younger children expressed fear but vocalised the prospect of death less assuredly than the older groups. Charlie tentatively suggested that 'I don't think they're going to kill me', whereas the older group most assuredly acknowledged that 'if they stab you...that's it'.

Following on, Ted (aged 15) introduces guns into the conversation and his fear that death may be sudden, violent and beyond his control. He clearly states that he is scared to die in this way. Although Hanusch (2008) argues that few studies have empirically examined just how visible death is in the Western media, he later indicates that some members of society, often those constructed as having less power, such as children, tend to be considered more newsworthy (Hanusch 2010). In particular, I suggest, if something bad happens. Walter et al. (1995) also concurs, that whilst only a minority of deaths get reported, those that do tend to be of an extraordinary kind. Therefore, the type of death that Ted fears, is clearly present in media representations but perhaps unlikely as a personal experience. Nevertheless, the script is salient and explored by the same boys in the following exchange.

Ted: I've brought like a gun, not a real one obviously, but like you could die by getting shot and I don't want to and it scares me.

SC: Do you think it's likely?

Syed: Well in modern society, yeah it's highly possible, especially in America [pause]. It's getting more likely here though.

John: I mean if you're standing around and a bunch of chavs come out of nowhere, you don't know, they might have guns or knives.

Syed: Yeah, it's like when we come back from football and all five of us are just walking down the street and some little child comes up, you can tell they are scared of us, cos we might seem like chavs to them.

John: It's like if they come up to you or say something to you it makes you like right anxious. Cos like me and my Grandma were walking along and this chav was following us and then he started shouting and having-a-go and I just kept walking and trying to ignore him, but I couldn't do anything.

Ted: I think everyone associates chavs with death really.

Syed: That's because we all want them to die [emotionally charged **voice**] [pause]

Ted: Yeah and the other way round. [Silence].

Syed: I mean like carrying knives shows disrespect for life somehow because I think a lot of people who carry knives might think it won't kill someone if they use it, but it will.

These boys clearly imply that the type of death described by Ted is 'highly probable'. The focus of concern is once again chavs and the unpredictable nature of violence, potentially death, associated by the boys to this group. The relationship between the boys in this study and the so-called chavs, highlights competing societal scripts in which the dual position of youth, as both threat and victim, is revealed. In an emotionally charged moment, Syed vehemently expresses his discomfort with the position of victim and forcefully announces that 'we' want 'them' [the chavs] to die. The following silence is somewhat uncomfortable, as the boys reflect on the impassioned essence of Syed's words. After some consideration, Tom thoughtfully responds that perhaps the chavs may feel the same way about them. Syed then distances himself slightly from his previous stance, questioning the motives of knife carriers and suggesting it shows a great disrespect for life, a script that is constantly available and attempts to place value on the lives and deaths of individuals. However, the prominent media depiction of knife crime combined with youth and fatality is, for Syed, persistent and all-consuming, and sadly his observations end in death.

The multiple cultural scripts surrounding young-people and knife crime are available through socially constructed impressions of childhood and death. Young-people are situated as threats [thugs, chavs] or innocent victims, death is sudden, brutal and violent, young-people are placed in the wrong place at the wrong time, death is a waste of 'young' lives. These positions are frequently played out through the television and news media and are clearly recognisable in these conversations. The young-people's interpretation of these complex scripts positions knife crime as very real and fearful prospect and a palpable threat to their own mortality.

In contrast to the previous group, where knives were seen as sudden and violent bringers of death in everyday circumstances, the following group, of a similar age, considered, developed and challenged the script of 'knife-equals-death'. The knife, although acknowledged as an object that could inflict death, was marvelled at by Andrew (aged 16) 'so many people have died through such a simple object', but was equally seen as something that cuts, changes and creates.

Andrew: I've got a knife, there's no blade in it fortunately.

Isaac (aged 15): [Holds up a craft knife and looks across at Andrew]. That's not a knife. [All laugh]

Andrew: You kept your blade in.

Isaac : Yeah, but I didn't take it to school.

Andrew: It just represents cutting things, knife crime, and the way so many people have died through such a simple object.

Isaac: Well I brought mine along, this knife here, well you can't see it on the tape but this is modelling knife that I use quite a lot. I bought ten of them for a pound from Poundland. They last for about thirty seconds before they disintegrate when I'm trying to cut through stuff [laughing].

James (aged 15): Did they sell them to you?

Isaac: Yeah.

Andrew: Yeah but I make models with them I don't stab people. [All laugh]

Isaac: Yeah but I make models with them I don't stab people. [All laugh]

SC: But they didn't know that in Poundland did they. [All laugh]

Isaac: Exactly. It's interesting though they do sell knives in France and Switzerland for example, in knife shops, and displayed in the window, where knife crime is not so, it's not part of the culture. My sister who is ten, actually bought a knife in France with her own pocket money to do whittling, to whittle down bits of wood at the campsite, but anyway that's just interesting about different cultures in different countries. But I use this craft knife to create different things with, to do modelling with, to cut pieces of wood and things. By cutting things, physically changing them with the knife you can build something that is bigger. So by destroying you can also create with the knife. So something which can kill things can also create others.

These boys acknowledged the cultural script of knife-equals-death but their ability to view the object from another perspective was clear, and therefore a more pragmatic approach dominated this exchange. Knives and knife crime were viewed through different scripts and alternatives were identified. Whilst an underlying understanding of the potential danger of knives to cause harm was present, a far more positive awareness was also demonstrated. Knives were discussed as objects that are forbidden in school and the purchase of them, to those under the age of 16 years, controlled by legislation. Therefore, a discourse of constraints and controls around the use of knives was discussed, issues that had not previously been mentioned by other groups. Furthermore, cultural differences concerning the use and purchase of knives were raised and explored, in opposition to the sole purpose being that of killing. Coombs argues that 'The key challenge to the violent knife crime script came through the emergence of the knife as an implement that cuts, changes and creates, [and therefore] not purely an object of destruction' (2014: 297).

Throughout these conversations the knife was used as an implement to explore young-people's mortality. It was positioned in different cultures and times, enabled feelings of uncertainty, anger and fear to be explored and was constructed as both killer and creator. To conclude this section, Jack (aged 16), further analyses the theme and its portrayal in the media. His response is critical of media scripts that portray all young-people as 'yobs' and is equally disparaging of the time afforded to such extraordinary deaths and consequently their rejection and censorship of more normal and usual deathways.

Jack: The final thing I've got in here is a knife, a paper one not a real one, because it makes you think of knife crime, and quite a lot of teenagers are dying because of knife crime, and then the media portrays all teenagers as yobs. I want to say that although some people may carry knives around not all teenagers are like that, and that some people who are like that are a bit weird. I think programmes try to jazz it all up a bit. Most deaths are really quite normal and nothing unusual happens but the media seems to want there to be a serial killer in every town, and everyone's going to die by falling off a cliff or getting stabbed.

It's All About Famous People Who Die

The dying and death of media celebrity Jade Goody was 'by far the most public in Britain' (Walter 2009: 2). Images of her dying dominated the front covers of the popular press for months. Scripts, both written and visual, alluded to the romance of her wedding, speculation about domestic violence, her heroism in the face of death, all intertwined with the constant images of her dying. In addition, splashes of glamour were added to the overall construction of a young woman dying of cancer. Seale (1998) highlights how the media and modern technology mediate personal experience within late modernity, leading to vicarious identification with media celebrities and their lives.

A number of recently deceased media celebrities were high on the agenda for discussion here, often linked to the dominant script of 'glamour' accompanying both celebrity lives and the rituals surrounding their deaths. Interestingly, a number of the young-people suggested that although the lives, and the subsequent eulogising, of well-known celebrities may include elements of glamour, their deaths were often less so. This was powerfully illustrated through Jade's dying of cervical cancer, Heath Ledger's overdose, Michael Jackson's overdose of prescribed medication and Alexander McQueen's suicide. Lucy (aged 15) begins by explaining McQueen's death.

> Lucy: This morning Alexander McQueen died, he killed **himself** because 3 weeks ago his Mum died and 3 years ago his best friend killed herself. I think it's quite a nasty chain of events to kill yourself because someone else has died, because everyone will be mourning each other and it's

very sad. Plus, I liked his clothes [Laughs. Hesitates]. I think it's a shame though that some people are going to be remembered more than others. It's unfair.

Lucy describes the suicide of McQueen; she is very matter-of-fact in her description and omits any mention of glamorous lifestyle. Instead she points to his death as 'sad' and 'nasty' due to the events leading up to it. The glamorous script, so often peddled in the media and liberally applied to celebrity culture is not evident here. What concerns Lucy is why he should be remembered more than other people. She goes on to explore the death of Jade Goody.

> **Lucy:** Yeah, it's like Jade Goody, when she died all the things that she did that were frowned upon in her life were immediately forgiven. I never really agreed with what she was doing like selling her story every 5 min and being so public and not really being famous for really doing anything important. But what she did during the time she was dying, where she publicised cervical cancer and increased the amount of women having smear tests etcetera. That was a good result.

Again Lucy takes quite a hard line. The way Jade conducted her life is frowned upon, whereas her health promotion message, which raised awareness of cervical cancer during the period of her dying, is seen as a form of redemption for her highly public life. McQueen's and Goody's lives and deaths may have been endlessly portrayed as glamorous within the media, and a heroic subtext of Jade's public dying illustrated daily, but such scripts were not apparent in the accounts of these young-people. These seem to have been totally disregarded for a more authentic, genuine type of death. Perhaps, having been brought up in an age of high profile celebrity culture and having been surrounded by emotional outpourings for remote unknown figures, these young-people desire to see through the façade and glitz of fame to a more authentic reality of death and dying.

Laura and Amy (both aged 15) continue this critical approach with reference to Michael Jackson's death. Amy comments, as did Lucy previously, that famous people get publicity when they die but ordinary people do not. This disparity seems to concern them.

Laura: There are lots of documentaries about people who have **died**, like Michael Jackson. [Mockingly] Oooooh he actually died.

Amy: It's all about publicity for famous people who die but there's no information about ordinary people who die.

Jack(aged 16): Well those sorts of deaths [celebrity] affect you more but other people less. I think it's because no-one knows, you just don't know them, so it would interest you less and no-one would be interested in it if 'so-and-so' died, and anyway there's too many people to mention everyone. So famous people you would be interested in because you've seen them in this or that and so you would be interested in what happens to them, but a person who lives a million miles away who you haven't heard of, or has done nothing special, would be insignificant to the general public.

The relationship between the visibility of celebrity deaths and someone less well known is discussed and reflected upon by the young-people. Jack considers that the impact of a celebrity death is largely as a result of high profile media representations, leading to a type of virtual intimacy, which does not occur in the invisible spaces of ordinary deaths. Celebrity lives and deaths are highly visible aspects of young-people's everyday lives and Hanusch (2010) observes that daily exposure to celebrities' lives, leaves people feeling like they know them, even though they have never met. Similarly, Kitch and Hume's claim that 'the mediated sharing of the stories of strangers' deaths may be the most common death experience in modern culture' (2008: xvii).

However, notwithstanding the above argument these young-people seemed disinterested and at times openly hostile to portrayals of celebrity death, suggesting they lack authenticity. If Kitch and Hume's supposition is correct and celebrity deaths are the most common experience of death in the Western world, is it possible that young-people are attempting to avoid mortality in their stringent denial of such events, or alternatively are they shunning the glamour to engage more fully in the reality of ordinary death? Is therefore the context of 'ordinary death' missing in their lives and can engagement with these types of death potentially plug the gap? It would seem not, as Amy seeks reassurance, commenting that 'there is no information about ordinary deaths'.

Although such high profile deaths, of which the young-people speak, occur in reality, they may be portrayed in a way that suggests unreality. The images appear confusing and the young-people appear to wrestle with these images of celebrity life and death. Whilst they clearly understand the 'realness' of these deaths, the context and the razzmatazz are less clear. Merrin suggests, in his evaluation of the media images of the death of Diana Princess of Wales in 1997, that 'the more we try to produce the real the more we threaten it' and that 'our attempts to produce the real only leave us more insecure' (1999: 59).

Despite their reservations, glamorous scripts and images of celebrity death were not to be completely erased from the conversations. Here, a slightly older group examined how death is glamorised through celebrity culture, fashion and the media, and exhibited more acceptance and less confusion at this.

Will (aged 17): [Holds up a picture of women in a black hat and **veil**]. It's kind of ...[hesitates]

Claire (aged 17): It looks like Lady Gaga from here.

Will: It's a veil. It represents to me how death is sort of glamorised in like magazines and films and on TV. They incorporate these glamorous elements like veils and fans and stuff.

Claire: They make death all like visual and everything. It's seen as like sexy, like all these supernatural programmes that make death look sexy, but at the end of the day it's like your body in the earth, and so it's not really that sexy, is it.

Mike (aged 17): Like why do we wear veils? Like, you wear a white veil when you get married and a black one for death.

Will: Well the white veil is for purity and virginity.

Mike: Ha, not in this day and age it's not. [All laugh].

Claire: **Well not many people wear white veils over their faces now.**

Paul (aged 17): No it's more like a diamante cluster. [All laugh again].

Claire: Yeah, what I mean is like all the vampire like films and stuff, and like fashion and the black veils and people like Lady Gaga, it's like very popular in the media at the moment. It's not the whole Gothic thing but more acceptable somehow. Books and films and stuff are full of it at the moment

This conversation features the glamorisation of death and dying in popular culture. Media coverage, which glamorises life and perhaps conversely death and dying, is something that these young-people are familiar with. This slightly older group were able to juggle the 'sexy' and often-unrealistic images with the knowledge that in reality death is not often like this. They appeared to do this more readily and with a greater sense of ease than the younger teenage groups who appeared somewhat confused by it. This group did not juxtapose 'ordinary' with 'celebrity' deaths, and did not question why these deaths were more apparent in the media. However, they amusingly illustrate that just as there are many different 'life-styles' there are also a number of 'death-styles', made obvious through the prominence of fashion, celebrity, literary and cinematic cultures. These are woven into the framework of young-people's everyday experiences and handled with dexterity.

Walter (2009) argues, that through the media, audiences have become more familiar with intimacies previously un-explored, and that those heretofore private, innermost and secret lives of families, celebrities and random chat show participants are now widely exhibited. To these, he suggests, we should now add the dying. Foltyn (2008: 170) equally observes, that our now shared grief and fascination of dead celebrities acts to familiarise society with death and corporeality. From these conversations, it would appear that young-people are certainly witnessing and sharing in the lives, loves and deaths of celebrities as part of their everyday experience. Some may see this as a positive step towards gaining more information about death and others may be more sceptical or distrustful, perhaps even confused by what they see. However, all gave the impression that they were able to question and scrutinise the charade so often paraded before them.

Finally in this chapter, Jo (aged 15) questions the authenticity behind the glamour of celebrity deaths, in particular appraising specific and prevalent iconic images. The portrayal of such deaths often contain a variety of cultural scripts, images and media representations, some of which are so deeply embedded in our understanding that we find them difficult to dispel. Whilst evaluating the fluidity and complexity of these ideas, images and thoughts, Jo iterates the differences between media constructions and the harsh realities of actual death.

> Jo: Celebrity deaths are no more important than anyone else's. Everybody dies, so why should the death of a celebrity be any more important than someone's grandma who died last week. I don't think they are glamorous; no one's death is glamorous. Apart from Marylyn Monroe of course. I thought her death was glamorous. I have an image of a Beverly Hills mansion or somewhere like that, and her lying on the bed with a bottle of sleeping pills. You think it must be glamorous because they are famous, but you know it wasn't really.

Conclusion

Walter (2009) argues rightly, that deaths are highly visible in the mass media, but those covered are often unusual and therefore not the kind that audiences are likely to face themselves. He comments that changing times mean that the dead paraded before us are not the traditional family dead but a,

> more heterogeneous bunch of heroes, historical figures, recent celebrities, and random family ancestors; characters found in museums, on the television news, and in genealogical web-sites; they range from prehistoric bog bodies to recently murdered children….(Walter 2008b: 4)

The four key scripts that dominated these conversations reinforce, I believe, Walter's ideas. The young-people constructed romantic, heroic, celebrity and violent narratives of death, which were in no way banal, understated or ordinary. Whilst McInerney (2009) stresses the oppositional nature of violent and romantic deaths, she emphasises the shared underpinning of the extraordinary and a dearth of ordinary deaths. This is something that young-people are clearly recognising for themselves.

This chapter has explored young-people's awareness of various different media representations of death and dying. They used the sources, stories and scripts gleaned from their environment to inform their understanding of and responses to death, and to tell their own stories via the material they brought with them. They explored, challenged, accepted, rejected, laughed at, feared and were silenced by the stories presented in the media, by their peers, and the interaction between the two. They read about death in books, the *Twilight* vampire series being particularly relevant in both written and cinematic forms to their accounts of death, the undead, and the glamorisation and sexualisation of death. Furthermore, newspapers, magazines and television reports allowed them to enter into the lives and deaths of celebrities and unknown people from around the world. These images and texts seem to have reassured them by providing accounts of social values or cultural practices, whilst continuing to romanticise, glamorise and sanitise the reality of death. As a result of media influence, claims for the sequestration of death can be challenged, as others have argued. Young—people find themselves surrounded by discourses of death and dying, whilst continually questioning and reflecting upon the authenticity and reality of such accounts.

Berridge questions if the witnessing of 'death as entertainment' is potentially 'conning us that we are getting up close to death, when in reality we have never been further away' (2002: 5). Television, she suggests, is 'the main medium that delivers this paradoxical perception of seeing things close up from a distance—an unreal reality' (2002: 5). However, as with all confidence tricks, it is the ability to see through them that prevents the individual from being duped. Although young-people are part of and participate in this unreal reality, they are clearly aware of its potential to deceive, and actively challenge a number of dominant cultural representations. It would seem that the differing forms of entertainment, as described by Berridge, rather than removing young-people from the reality of death actually encourage them to reach out beyond the boundaries imposed by the media, accepting or rejecting such discourses, and incorporating and expressing their own lived experience. They may not have encountered the natural death of a close relative or friend but their narratives indicate that when they do they will be aware of what it is and the varied possibilities of response.

These conversations demonstrate a diversity of childhoods and a multiplicity of possible deathways. They highlight personal understanding and active agency through the construction of, and reflection upon, death-related examples. They distinguish approaches to gender-related accounts of death, highlight abilities of moral reasoning, illustrate risks within society, and intertwine imagined and real deaths via the recognition of dominant media scripts in their own lives. Furthermore, the ability to learn about death by challenging, adopting and adapting these scripts is clear. The romantic and celebrity scripts were often seen as unreal and unauthentic, the heroic scripts contained elements that were to be aspired to, and the violence and uncertainty of scripts relating to knife crime were both feared and rationalised. The very sources, stories and scripts that are often accused of adding mystery, rather than reality to death, seem to be demystified and made more real through the accounts of these young-people. It is clear that whilst a teenage girl in a T-shirt is just one depiction of death to the young-people in my study, death actually comes in many and various everyday guises.

References

Armstrong-Coster, A. (2005). In morte media Jubilate [2]: A study of cancer-related pathographies. *Mortality, 10*(2), 97–112.

Becker, E. (1973). *The denial of death*. New York: The Free Press.

Berridge, K. (2002). *Vigor mortis*. London: Profile Books.

Blackman, M. (2007). *The stuff of nightmares*. London: Doubleday.

Boden, N. (2007). *Knife crime every 24 seconds*. http://www.independent.co.uk/news/uk/crime/knife-crime-every-24-minutes-398149.html. Accessed May 11 2011.

Bronfen, E. (1992). *Over her dead body: Death femininity and the aesthetic*. Manchester University Press: Manchester.

Buckingham, D. (2011). *A manifesto for media education*. http://www.manifestoformediaeducation.co.uk/2011/01/mdia-education-should-be-3/. Accessed February 28 2011.

Coombs, S. (2014). Death wears a T-shirt: Listening to young people talk about death. *Mortality, 19*(3), 284–302.

Dixon-Woods, M., Seale, C., Young, B., Findlay, M., & Heney, D. (2003). Representing childhood cancer: Accounts from newspapers and parents. *Sociology of Health & Illness, 25*(2), 143–164.

Earle, S., & Komaromy, C. (2009). Death and dying in poetry, fiction and the media. In S. Earle, C. Bartholomew, & C. Komaromy (Eds.), *Making sense of death, dying and bereavement: An anthology*. London: Sage.

Foltyn, J. L. (2008). Dead famous and death sexy: Popular culture. *Forensics, and the rise of the Corpse, Mortality, 13*(2), 153–173.

Giddens, A. (1991). *Modernity and self-identity: Self and society in the late modern age*. Cambridge: Polity Press.

Gorer, G. (1955). The pornography of death. *Encounter.* October.

Hallam, E., & Hockey, J. (2001). *Death, memory and material culture*. Oxford: Berg.

Hanusch, F. (2008). Graphic death in the news media: Present or absent? *Mortality, 13*(4), 301–317.

Hanusch, F. (2010). *Representing death in the news: Journalism, media and mortality*. Basingstoke: Palgrave Macmillan.

Hockey, J., Komaromy, C., & Woodthorpe, K. (2010). Recovering presence. In J. Hockey, C. Komaromy, & K. Woodthorpe (Eds.), *The matter of death: Space, place and materiality*. Palgrave MacMillan: Basingstoke.

Howarth, G. (2007). *Death and dying: A sociological introduction*. Cambridge: Polity Press.

James, A., Jenks, C., & Prout, A. (1998). *Theorizing childhood*. Cambridge: Polity Press.

Kitch, C., & Hume, J. (2008). *Journalism in a culture of grief*. New York: Routledge.

Knox, S. L. (2006). Death. *Afterlife, and the Eschatology of Consciousness: Themes in Contemporary Cinema, Mortality, 11*(3), 233–252.

Livingstone, S. (2009). *Children and the Internet*. Cambridge: Polity Press.

Mayall, B. (2002). *Towards a sociology for childhood: Thinking from children's lives*. Buckingham: Open University Press.

McInerney, F. (2009). Cinematic visions of dying. In A. Kellehear (Ed.), *The Study of dying: From autonomy to transformation*. Cambridge: Cambridge University Press.

Merrin, W. (1999). Crash, Bang, Wallop! What a Picture! *The Death of Diana and the Media, Mortality, 4*(1), 41–62.

Postman, N. (1982). *The disappearance of childhood*. New York: Vintage Books.

Prout, A. (2005). *The future of childhood: Towards the interdisciplinary study of children*. Abingdon: RoutledgeFalmer.

Russell, B. (2009). *One third of children admit to carrying a gun or knife*. http://www.independent.co.uk/news/uk/crime/one-third-of-children-admit-to-carrying-a-gun-or-knife-1638512.html. Accessed May 11 2011.

Seale, C. (1995). Heroic death. *Sociology, 29*(4), 597–613.

Seale, C. (1998). *Constructing death: The sociology of dying and bereavement*. Cambridge: Cambridge University Press.

Sontag, S. (1978). *Illness as Metaphor*. London: Penguin.

Walter, T. (2008a). The sociology of death. *Sociology compass, 2*(1), 317–336.

Walter, T. (2008b). The presence of the dead in society. A Paper Presented at the Conference on Death and Dying in 18-21c Europe, Alba Iulia, Romania. http://www.bath.ac.uk/cdas/research/. Accessed July 22 2012.

Walter, T. (2009). Jade's dying body: The ultimate reality show. *Sociological Research Online, 14*(5), 3.1. Retrieved May 27th 2011, from http://www.socresonline.org.uk/14/5/1.html. Accessed May 27 2011.

Walter, T., Littlewood, J., & Pickering, M. (1995). Death in the news: The public invigilation of private emotion. *Sociology, 29*, 579–596.

Weinstein, J. (2002). Teaching and Learning About Loss. In N. Thompson (Ed.), *Loss and grief: A guide for human services practitioners*. Palgrave: Hampshire.

4

Letting Death Out of the Box

Introduction

Holden Caulfield, teenager and main protagonist in Salinger's novel *The Catcher in the Rye* (1951) contemplates death. His hope is to be 'dumped' in a river rather than end up in a cemetery with flowers on his chest. 'Who wants flowers when you're dead'? he asks, 'Nobody' is his firm reply (1951: 140). The conversations in this chapter, in a similar way to Holden's own reflections, examine young-people's distinctive and sometimes quirky views on and experiences of death and death rituals. The tangible nature and emotional connectedness to the materiality of death is exposed and helps to position no topic as out of reach; even insights into their own deaths. Unavailable to Holden in the 1950s, the highly accessible spaces for on-line knowledge and memorialisation are also considered in some detail.

The previous chapter examined how young-people interact with a variety of highly public media sources and how these help them form relationships with death on an everyday basis; death at a safe distance perhaps. In contrast this chapter brings death 'up-close-and-personal'

© The Author(s) 2017
S. Coombs, *Young People's Perspectives on End-of-Life*,
Studies in Childhood and Youth, DOI 10.1007/978-3-319-53631-6_4

as it encounters death through individual experiences, personal memories, the loss of meaningful relationships and the importance of objects both physical and virtual to remembering. Individual narratives of death, dying and loss are constructed less overtly via cultural scripts, as discussed in the previous chapter, but more intimately by and through the self. However, the boundaries between the two realms of public and private are blurred and permeable, and therefore personal reflections continue to draw from dominant representations in order to elaborate upon private experience. Therefore, the framework of sources, stories, scripts and 'stuff', as discussed in the previous chapter, continues to be useful, as both public and private elements combine in the appreciation of young-people's stories.

Memorialisation and material culture are fundamental to this chapter and central to symbolising death in everyday life. For example, a walk around my hometown reveals several church graveyards, a cemetery, a roadside memorial and a signpost to a historical burial site; spaces that commemorate both the long and recently dead. My home contains an ornament that belonged to my Grandfather, my Grandmother's wedding ring and photographs of dead relatives, all of whom continue to be remembered by us and live with us. Hockey et al. emphasize the enduring presence of the dead through remaining material objects in everyday places and how these help to 'make sense of more mysterious or abstract domains' (2010: 7). The utilisation of objects for this very purpose is clearly evident in the conversations that follow, similarly highlighting the importance of relationships between people and their material environments. Notwithstanding the significance of physical memento mori, young-people also connect with virtual forms of memorialisation, which provide opportunities to share ideas, feelings and secrets through blogs and websites. Having travelled with death from public sources to private stories and into cyberspace, these material objects also uncover the ways in which some of these young-people might wish to be remembered, and like Holden, it's not often with flowers of their chest.

Following the themes described above, personal encounters with death provide valuable memories and play a significant role in the everyday lives of these young-people. Clearly evidenced by the stories they tell, the material objects they treasure, the online secrets they share, and the inventive possibilities they perform in relation to their own future death rituals. In as much as young-people enter into a world of visual images and texts that bring multiple representations of death into their lives, they also exist in a world of physical relationships, love and loss. In this world, Hockey et al. (2010) propose that death relates to many things; disposal rituals, memorials, places, objects, mourning, and therefore all the 'stuff' that surrounds the ending of an embodied life. These conversations reveal this diversity of experience and response, which in part negates the universality of physical and emotional pain so often described, and so repeatedly used by adults as the raison d'être for not talking to the young about death in the first place. Young-people may use sources and scripts that relate to societal influences surrounding the end-of-life but they also use stories and stuff of a more highly personal nature. Death is brought into sharp focus through their individual narratives, material and virtual memorials, and the rehearsal of their own end-of-life rituals. These everyday stories uncover and give life to a 'bigger picture' of what dying, death and end-of-life rituals mean to these young-people. That this knowledge can only ever be partial is accepted. However, reflecting on these stories, once again challenges deeply held convictions that death belongs to a 'kingdom of childhood', where nobody ever dies, [nobody that matters that is].

Stories for Telling

Young-peoples' stories and experiences are given prominence in this book in order to display the many ways in which death is encountered in their everyday lives and provide a self-evident variety of responses to death and the rituals surrounding it. Telling their stories, literally and metaphorically lets, or more assertively 'gets', death out of the box, allowing previously private and untold accounts to be aired and shared. The presentation of significant, personal experience, by way of a narrative format, illuminates the importance of these events, not only for themselves but equally for their listening friends. Young-people, as with adults, are not an homogenous group who respond to death in the same way. Pollock (1990) argues that narratives help us to make sense of experience and in conjunction provide us with meaning, both of ourselves and the world in which we live. Particularly poignant, is Pollock's further suggestion that, 'the narrative act entails garnering the past for an ephemeral present and an infinitely unstable future' (1990: 3).

Seale argues that the 'human experience of death allows us to understand some fundamental features of social life' (1998: 1). In encountering, experiencing and telling their stories these young-people connect with the embodied nature and finality of life, they explore their own individual responses to death, and likewise the influence of dominant cultural reactions. Relationships, both in life and in continuing bonds with the dead, influence how such encounters help to construct meaning in the face of death. That death poses existential problems for humans is a commonly held view and young-people are no exception to that. Perhaps their youth gives them a distance from death, not so readily available to those of more advanced years, or as I argue, it allows them to communicate their ideas of death and dying with a greater clarity and certainty, commonly denied adults.

Therefore, the initial focus of this chapter is on young-people's first-hand encounters with death. Such events bring death a step closer, making it more personal and intimate, whilst concurrently encouraging the exchange and sharing of ideas. Frank suggests that stories always pose the listener with the question, 'what kind of truth is being told' here, and although stories themselves cannot resolve this dilemma, their work is 'to remind us that we have to live with complicated truths' (2010: 5). That many and complex truths are present in these stories is therefore not to be wondered at but rather treasured and appreciated.

'Dear Harold' and Others

After media representations, as discussed in the last chapter, some of the first encounters young-people experience of actual death, and therefore their own responses to the finality of life, relate to pets. Whilst Valentine (2006) explored the lasting impact of human loss and bereavement on the lives of individuals, Kaufman and Kaufman (2006) studied the importance and consequences of childhood pet bereavement. Young-people, from across the age range, spent a significant amount of conversation-time telling stories of the loss, usually but not exclusively, of 'much loved' pets. A variety of encounters, responses and ritual practices are uncovered, which provide the opportunity to explore death and loss from the young participants own, widely held views, that pet deaths offer valuable learning opportunities for the future. Machin sees these everyday situations as 'little' losses, situating them within a framework of 'rehearsals for more profound encounters with loss' and suggesting they 'provide a strengthening of the emotional and cognitive capacities for dealing with grief' (2009: 3).

Laura and Amy (both aged 15), provide some amusing accounts of the deaths of various pets that occurred when they were younger. The performance, by Laura, of the dead rat was a source of great entertainment, as was Amy's impersonation of her Mother when she realised, what the young child did not, that the pet rabbit was in fact dead and not asleep. These two witty enactments enhanced the vibrancy of the stories and in turn heightened their significance for the tellers and the told. Notwithstanding the humorous elements, the emotional impact and evidence of touching responses also came to the fore.

Laura: My rabbit died when I was about 5, and then my guinea pigs died, but I wasn't so much bothered about them because I didn't really like them. [All laugh]. But then my brother's rat died and because he found it, he was more upset because he like walked into the room and she [the rat] was just lying there on her back like that [Laura puts hands in the air and tilts her head backwards] … [everyone laughs] … in the bottom of the cage, and he just sat at the front of the cage like gazing at her [she gazes forward, eyes wide] … [everyone laughs]

Amy: Yes, like shocked. I found my rabbit [names rabbit] dead in the morning and I thought he was asleep. I was like, 'Mum, [names rabbit] asleep and not moving', and she's like, [shakes her head and changes her voice to imitate her Mother's knowing response]. 'I don't think he is Amy'. [All laugh]. So that was quite upsetting, but we did like the whole funeral thing, and Dad dug a hole, and I cried throughout the whole of that. My Mum and Dad said we couldn't have any pets after that because we were so upset when they died, and I was like, well yeah, but it showed me that death happens and made it more realistic

Differing reactions are evident although a pervading sense of humour is acknowledged and welcomed. Potentially these responses could be viewed as a way of handling the emotionality of such situations, or alternatively the ability of young-people to react to death with a sense of amusement. That death can elicit this kind of response is seldom explored, as concerns around the sensitivity of the topic are usually paramount. Notably, death is seen to produce universal reactions such as pain and anguish and therefore the potential for various other responses is largely discounted. Perhaps, it is possible to suggest here that young-people can and do juggle multiple meanings and reactions to the death of pets and humans alike, and that failing to explore these, due to preconceived notions of inflicting emotional trauma, discourages adults from engaging with young-people on this topic.

Putting aside humour, the emotional impact of pet deaths, the shock often felt at sudden loss, and the ritual burying with 'full honours,' were also noted by many of the young-people. The suggestion that pet deaths provide an opportunity to understand the nature of death prior to what they identify as 'far sadder future events' (Isaac aged 15), was frequently talked about, as can be seen in Isaac's story of his goldfish, Harold.

Isaac   : Pets are a good way of introducing children to this [death], because it's obviously very sad but may prepare them for far sadder future events. I mean I've had too many pets I think, chickens, goldfish [hesitates]… Harold. Dear Harold, I couldn't put him in the box. We had him for three years, he was an epic goldfish, but one day he decided he'd had enough and that was it. It was very sad but I did learn that pets don't last forever [hesitates]… and neither do people

Isaac's sadness at the loss of his pet is evident but his recognition that potentially sadder deaths would be encountered is equally clear, as was the case in Laura and Amy's previous discussion. Retrospectively, Isaac equates the death of his goldfish as an opportunity to learn about the finality of life and extends these ideas from his pet to people. The culmination of many of these pet stories was as a precursor to preparing for 'real' deaths.

The emotional intensity of many of these pet stories came about through acknowledging the reactions of others. Young-people pointed out that those around them often influenced their responses to such deaths. Mike (aged 17), and Jack (aged 16) demonstrate the importance of parental reactions.

> **Mike:** My cat got put down while I was on holiday in Portugal, having a good time. And I don't think any of you have ever seen my Dad but he's like a man [emphasises word 'man'], you know a real man, a very big man, and his head's shaved and everything and my Mum was telling me that my Dad was just crying, and they were in Morrison's and Dad was just crying and I've never seen my Dad cry, ever

Jack's story is similar.

> **Jack:** For me, when my pet died that made me upset, so my parents got upset and that was hard, because I always see my parents as the ones who look after me and are strong and then when I see them upset it makes me feel …[short silence]
>
> **Amy** (aged 15): Terrible
>
> **Jack:** A bit sad, yeah. [Long Silence]

The emotionality of parents is seen as difficult to cope with. The death of the pet is almost secondary to the emotional response of the parents and the impact this has on the young-person. Mike highlights the masculine nature of his Father, his size, his shaved head, and contrasts this with the story his Mother has told him about his Father crying. To Mike this is a somewhat incongruous event, he finds the image of his tearful Father difficult to reconcile with his own construction of him as a 'man', plus the added context of a public place. Jack equally finds his parents being upset as disconcerting and unsettling.

Young-people's narratives of pet deaths showed an eclectic mix of views and responses ranging from trauma and sadness to humour and relief. That animals play a large part in family life and therefore when they die bring death a step closer is undeniable. That pets link with a variety of death related human responses in also pertinent, as Paul concludes,

Paul (aged 17): Speaking of pets I was completely not bothered when my dog died. In fact, I was quite happy because I didn't have to walk the smelly old thing anymore.

Nothing Is Quite the Same

Whilst pets are an important part of young-people's lives and sometimes the only close death they encounter during their teenage years, many may experience the death of a grandparent, fellow pupil or family friend. Indeed, these discussions uncovered many detailed encounters of this type, in and through which, as suggested by Valentine, grief's bigger picture was revealed through the complexity of 'human relationships' and the process of 'meaning making' (2006: 58). The stories highlight differences in experiences of death and grief; sometimes confusion, often continuing bonds and evocative memories, or feelings of powerlessness and/or agency, all were evident in these meetings with death, grief and the rituals surrounding it. Valentine (2008), equally argues that attempts to understand human experiences of grief and loss cannot be accomplished through overarching and general terms. Rather, that discursive activities highlight more readily the ways in which people encounter death, as they provide opportunities for very different pictures to emerge, away from the constraints and formalities of prescribed forms of grieving. Therefore, in order to try and understand, and to capture how death, loss and grief are played out in the everyday lives of these young-people it was important to listen to and examine their own unique stories. Justine begins this section by suggesting that after death 'nothing is quite the same'.

Justine (aged 11): Well this one says [holds up a piece of paper] 'nothing is quite the same', because when someone dies like my Grandma [name] things are never the same after that. Every week on a Saturday afternoon we went to see her and now we can't but we just have to go on without her and it's sad in a way because I miss her … and we got her ashes [long silence]. It's just like little things that are missing. Not now so much but when she did die there was something missing. Like when she died my Mum asked me if I wanted to go to the funeral but I didn't want to, I stayed with some friends, I made a picture though [for Grandma], and the picture went to funeral instead of me.

Justine's account emphasises her response to her Grandmother's death, her sadness in acknowledging that her life has changed, and her longing to see her Grandmother again whilst still coming to terms with life without this key relationship. In contemporary Western society these are dominant cultural scripts that link closely with everyday feelings and responses to death and bereavement.

That young-people can only manage death in this way is unlikely in the context of the everyday and fast changing world in which they exist. Machin argues that contemporary life and death are situated in a world where new possibilities for creating, extending and ending life occur, this will be explored further in the next chapter, and that the 'perceptions and understanding about life and death issues reflect the social climate in which they take place' (2009: 3). It would be impossible to ignore the social and cultural phenomena that impact on young-people's encounters with death, but equally the rich diversity of response inhibits the homogenisation of the impact of death on the young. Mike (aged 17), looks back at his first encounter with death, at the age of 14, and explores the social context of the dying, death and funeral of his Godmother. Although this death had occurred 3 years previously the memories remain vivid, and for him the experience was far from positive. His narrative constructs a clear picture of the alienating space in which his Godmother died, the intrusive medical interventions that did little to alleviate her suffering, the responses of relatives, and his own confusion at what was happening in the final stages of her life. He indicates his understanding that 'it was her time to go' but how 'awful' this death and the funeral that followed were for him.

Mike: My Godmother, she died in like 2005. She had cancer, like lung cancer, and she was in a lot of pain and she was in hospital. I won't set foot in that hospital now because they were awful to her. I mean I know she was really thin but she did try to eat, and over the last months of her life I did watch her try to force down food but she sort of lived off black coffee and a banana each day. When she died we'd left the hospital. We left about 12 at night and she passed away about 20 past 12 in the morning. It was her time to go and I knew it was, but it was really awful. The last time I saw her, and I wished I hadn't gone, she was hooked up to a morphine drip, an oxygen mask, and every time she took a breath her head flew to the side and it … [stops, shakes his head, sighs]. And when we stood up to go and I was holding her hand and I kissed her forehead but she like grabbed my hand, like she knew we were there. It was awful, and I woke up in the morning to Mum crying and she said like [name] is dead. I was like… oh ok. It may sound a bit weird but when I'm upset and stuff I still talk to her and stuff [silence]. Well, then she [refers to his Godmother] had a funeral, and she had two brothers, who didn't like her to be honest, but she was very religious, strongly Roman Catholic, but they like planned a humanist funeral. We couldn't believe it, and my Mum who was like her best friend was just furious with them, because [name] always said she wanted like a proper Catholic funeral, like done properly, and it was awful. The guy who did it like stood up and said stuff that he didn't need to say and he didn't know her and it was a really awful funeral. Really sad because that's not what she wanted.

Mike's first encounter with a significant and meaningful death is, as portrayed through his story telling, harsh and perhaps not what he had expected. It contrasts starkly with the humorous accounts of pet deaths or the romantic and heroic deaths portrayed by the media and discussed in the previous chapter. Mike finds this encounter with death difficult, the place of dying, the way of dying, the reality of dying and the family disagreements that ensued were, to him, really 'sad' and really 'awful'. His memories of this last meeting with his Godmother led him to say he 'wished he hadn't gone'; however, the memory of their final kiss and her 'gripping' his hand were taken as an acknowledgement of her awareness of his presence. His response to the knowledge of her death, when it came the following morning, was somewhat matter-of-fact, and to some extent secondary to his evaluation of the dying process. Mike's encounter with dying, death and death rituals demonstrated his confusion and anger at the adults' dealing with it, from both medical and family perspectives. Timmermans discusses how the medical and allied professions broker death for the relatives through their interventions and practices, in order that 'death is made useful for the living' (2005: 1007). Whether this was extended to the experience and presence of a

14-year-old boy is not clear. What is evident however is that despite the reality of his Godmother's death, a strong bond remains between them, which Mike emphasises by his ongoing dialogue with her. Valentine (2008) demonstrates how narratives of dying often contain similar elements to those presented by Mike; medical settings, intimacy, the unique qualities of the dying person, the relationships [sometimes good and sometimes not] with others, and the continuing bond. More specifically she suggests that 'In particular, dying moments celebrated the enduring nature of both personhood and the social bond' (2008: 164).

Lucy (aged 15) was faced with a similar situation to Mike; her Great Grandmother was dying of cancer in hospital. She demonstrates both resilience and strength of character in her response to both the death and to the views of the adults around her, in particular her Grandmother. Unlike Mike, who had been at the bedside of his Godmother in the dying moments of her life, and suggested that he wished he had not, Lucy refused to go, despite considerable pressure from her Grandmother.

Lucy: The only real close person that I have known to die was technically my Step Great Grandma, but I called her Nanna because I grew up with her being my Grandma. She got bowel cancer and died just before her 100th birthday. I was told by my Grandmother, her daughter, that I was 'evil' for not going to see her in hospital.

Jo (aged 15): Evil!

Lucy: Yes, but the reason why was because…. Was that my Mother had been the day before, and my brother wasn't allowed to go because he was too young, he was 10. But my Grandmother asked me to go, but I said 'no' because she [Nanna] would have been in the hospital ward, really ill, with her nightdress on, and wouldn't have had her hair done, wouldn't have had her teeth in, be incredibly ill, didn't remember her daughter, so she wouldn't have remembered me, and I preferred to remember her as the little old lady pottering around the garden, running round doing this and that, rather than remember a woman who was dying. I think that helped me to remember her, because instead of remembering a dying woman, I remembered my Nanna, who the day after her hip operation let go of her Zimmer frame and threw it away.

Lucy was clear and strong in her reasons for staying away from this scene. She created a vivid picture of how she wanted to remember her Great Grandmother, and her account reflects her own individuality and the much cherished strength of character of her 'Nanna'; perhaps indicative of their similar characteristics. Her imagined picture of the hospitalised death, which she refuses to be a part of, mirrors the actuality of Mike's experience. However, her own personal and special memories encapsulate her way of remembering the individuality and idiosyncratic nature of her Great Grandmother, which she feels helped her to overcome the loss.

The Body

Finally, in this section Peter (aged 15) tells the story of the dying and death of his Grandfather, and furthermore his encounter with the dead body. In a time when perhaps few adults, let alone young-people, meet with death so directly, Peter's experience is important, and brings the reality and the corporeality of death much closer to him. Interestingly, the sharing of his story also had a noticeable effect on the other boys in the group, who deftly create another narrative for Peter, in which the death of his Grandad is transformed into something good. Perhaps for their friend's sake, as Peter was clearly unsettled by his experience, they suggest that his Grandfather's suffering is now over and he is at peace. Peter hardly has time to reflect upon these suggestions, as the new story is promptly constructed, turning Peter's narrative into something different.

Peter: It really sort of brings it home when you see somebody die, like when you see a dead body.

SC: Have you seen a dead body Peter?

Peter: Yeah... well my Grandad. Well ...For me it was like worse when he was really ill, it was like it was still him but it wasn't. Seeing the body was like really weird, if it had been just some sort of guy it might have been different, but it really brought it home like. [Silence].

Chris (aged 14): Was it sort of nice though in a way though, cos you could see he wasn't suffering

Peter: Well… [Hesitates].

Chris: Like, he was like peaceful.

Peter: Well, I suppose, kind of… [Hesitates further].

Chris: Yeah, cos you don't want people to suffer.

Syed (aged 15): And like cancer is an awful thing cos it can kill you slowly. So it's a good thing really.

In a similar way, Valentine (2008), in her research with bereaved adults, notes how in conversations of this type that the socially constructed nature of personhood becomes apparent throughout the discussion, as appeared here, and the story narrator literally creates a space and a presence for the dead within the conversation encounter itself.

These stories demonstrate the rich diversity of accounts and encounters with death that these young-people experience. The stories told, literally open the box on death and the role of the dead in their everyday lives. The descriptions uncover the complex nature of death within everyday life and the ability of these young-people to reflect upon their own individual responses and those of the people around them. As Valentine suggests, dying is seldom presented as 'wholly good or wholly bad, but rather as full of ambiguity' (2008: 173). That death is part of young-people's lives is clear, likewise that it is experienced at close quarters and encounters with it are fairly common. These stories reveal the complexity, uncertainty and changing nature of death. They also illustrate ways in which young-people negotiate and explore such issues, by taking bold steps towards death, they develop their own personal meanings around it and involvement with it.

Objects for Remembering: Memento Mori

Encounters with death come in many forms and therefore, the stories just told, help to illuminate such meetings through insubstantial yet vital memories. However, encounters can also be expressed through the concrete physicality of material objects that contain memories of the dead. Howarth suggests 'it would appear that the dead might continue to have social presence amongst the living' (2007: 189), and this would certainly seem to be the case in the constant reminders of the dead that these young-people exhibited. Gillis notes that, 'monuments and cemeteries constitute a significant part of the modern landscape', but that, 'we also provide space for the dead closer to home, turning our residences into mini-mausoleums, featuring the photos and mementos of the deceased, refusing to let them depart' (1997: 202). Thus, as suggested by Hallam and Hockey, through 'ordinary' and 'mundane' deaths 'we analyse the everyday contexts of memory making' (2001: 1).

Young-people are no exception in the keeping of memento mori and were keen to show and share the stories behind the objects. These included photographs, swimming medals, a ceramic bell, the words of songs and poems, cuff links, Granddad's ashes, and many others. Many of the objects had belonged to dead relatives and friends and had been given as a keepsake, but many were everyday objects that the young-person associated with a deceased family member, and therefore evoked memories of that person. One of the most emotional and deeply meaningful moments within the study was when Ruth (aged 15) brought a small ceramic object out of her box and told its story.

> **Ruth:** [Places small blue ceramic dolphin on the table and speaks quietly and slowly, whilst touching the dolphin]. I have this dolphin thing that someone who died gave me. It was my Uncle [name] and I was about 7 [looks upset and gazes at the dolphin. Silence].
>
> [Everyone is clearly moved by this short announcement and remain silent too].
>
> **Ruth continues:** I'll always keep it. So yeah. [She looks down at the dolphin for a while and continues to touch it, then moves on to next item].

Gibson describes how 'in the most simple, fleeting and poignant moments, people grieve with and through objects' (2004: 296). This indeed was all of those; simple, fleeting and poignant, yet the emotional impact on everyone in the group was tangible. Ruth's quiet demeanour, frequent silences and body language spoke more loudly than her brief words. Everyone present appeared moved by this short account. The emotional impact of the object and Ruth's connection with it was very powerful.

Mixed emotions were apparent when Will (aged 17) brought out a piece of paper, on which he had composed a poem for his Grandmother's funeral.

Will: Recently my Nan died of Alzheimer's so I thought I'd bring something related to that. I couldn't actually carry her ashes here, which have recently been returned from the crematorium in a lovely purple plastic bag. [All laugh].

Paul (aged 17): Was it a River Island bag?

Will: [Will smiles] Well, to carry on. Instead of bringing my Nan, cos I didn't really want to carry her around college all day. You'd feel a bit weird carrying around your dead Grandma all day.

Paul: Imagine if you lost her. [All laugh].

Will: Yeah well that'd go down a treat. Well instead I brought the words I said at her funeral, and what a cracking funeral it was. [All laugh]. I brought, well I can't write poetry to save my life, so you know you can get little notes that you send to people and on cards there's like pre written poems, well I kinda smushed together some of those, and it kind of reminded me who she was. There's a line somewhere [searches for line], 'the hours that we spent just drinking cups of tea, I think of the advice you gave and the knowledge you would share'. It's the kind of thing that would represent her. It's probably why I drink so much tea now. I read it out in church, she was like a really close person to me, she was like a second Mum.

Will indicates that in order to write the poem he used some of his own words and some that he found in cards that were sent after his Nan died. He found the words quite moving and used them as a framework to compose his poem. Hallam and Hockey (2001: 175) briefly explore the use of sympathy cards describing them as 'ephemeral' forms of memorialisation or 'vernacular texts', unconstrained by institutional forms. Despite the lack of restrictions placed upon such forms of writing, Hallam and Hockey point out that they often draw upon more traditional forms such as literature, religious imagery or funeral rites to articulate emotions, reactions and sympathies and are therefore 'woven into and occupy spaces between the formalized rituals that surround death (2001: 175).

Will's poem fits well with these descriptions, and his reading of it moved everyone present.

Will reads: 'Words for Nan'

Life is not the same without you.
The sun still rises in the East and darkness falls at night
But nothing seems quite the same, each day is not as bright.
The birds still sing, the flowers grow, the breeze still whispers too
But it will never, ever be the same world without you.
It's so sad that you had to go; your leaving caused such pain
But you were special and earth's loss was heavens gain.
Nan I miss you.
I think of the joy you gave to others and the love that you shared too.
The happiness surrounding you and thoughtful things you do.
I think about the fun we had and times you sat me on your knee.
The hours we'd just sit chatting whilst drinking cups of tea.
I think of the advice you gave and knowledge you would share.
The warmth that always filled the room whenever you were there.
I think of all the memories and happy times together
The kindness you brought into my life will stay in my heart forever.
These few words don't seem adequate; it's difficult to say
How much you meant and how you're missed on every single day.
For you were really wonderful and all the world could see
That you were loved so very much, that's how you'll always be.

Due to the emotive content and Will's equally emotional response to it, he reflects upon the difficulties he faced when trying to vocalise the poem at the funeral. However, having been asked by his family to carry out the reading he does not want to 'let anyone down' and subsequently felt a sense of achievement at having accomplished a difficult but heartfelt and much needed expression of love and loss for his family. Machin suggests that reading other people's work can provide 'solace' and writing itself can be therapeutic, providing 'new perspectives and meaning' (2009: 69). Will was able to reflect upon and express his feelings for his Grandmother via this poem.

Having examined Ruth's blue dolphin and Will's 'Words for Nan' we now move on to take a look at some photographs. Sontag suggests that we live in a world of non-stop imagery but claims that that 'when it comes to remembering, the photograph has the deeper bite' (2003: 19). In a week when a huge number of photographs have depicted the mass death of young-people at a Norwegian summer camp on every newspaper front cover, the pivotal nature of talking to young-people about death seems relevant and poignant. Sontag elevates photographs to 'objects of contemplation', 'secular icons', 'memento mori' and suggests that their position as such requires an equally 'sacred or meditative space' in which to view them. This, she contends, 'is hard to come by in modern society, whose chief model of a public space is the mega-store' (2003: 107). Although I would not want to go so far as to claim my kitchen table as a 'sacred' space, it was, as previously discussed, the site for the majority of these conversations, and I feel it provided a place for contemplation of the photographs and objects that young-people conjured out of their boxes. Photographs were a common item, and were the source of many conversations, revealing the strength of attachment and feelings of loss in relation to the people within them. Jo, aged 15, brought one such photograph.

Jo: [Shows a photo from her box]. That's [uses name]. She was like the first real encounter I had with death. She was like the first person I really knew and like really loved in some ways that died. It was like, 'Oh my God [name] is dead'! I remember my Mum coming home; cos [name] lived at the nursing home where my Mum used to work, and Mum telling me. It was like 'argh'! I remember standing outside with my brother and sister and sobbing uncontrollably and they were both really upset too. It was like really hard because I thought, this is weird, and I'm never going to see her again. On the back of this photo [name] has written, 'I am now only afraid of being forgotten by everyone I know on Earth, only that', and I think that a lot of people may feel like that. Maybe they're not afraid of the whole actually snuffing-it lark, but that they will be forgotten. So sometimes you do forget people and you think how can I do that, but this photo means I'll never forget [name].

This photograph was clearly significant to Jo. Through it she recalls a friend, the importance of their relationship and the ongoing nature of that relationship. The photograph provides continuity and the message written on the back poignantly highlights this.

The objects described so far were deliberately chosen by these young-people as reminders of relationships that continue to evoke feelings and meanings in their everyday lives. However, sometimes memories can come to us unbidden, 'sometimes stimulated inadvertently within the flow of our embodied encounters in the material world' (Hallam and Hockey 2001: 105). Isaac illustrates how an everyday item reminds him of his Grandmother.

> **Isaac** (aged 15): My Grandma died recently and whenever I see a teacake, you know the chocolate marshmallow things with the cardboard bottom that taste horrible, she used to feed them to us as a 'treat' whenever we visited her house, and so I associate those with her quite a lot and it does make me think of Grandma. I was very sad because that was the first experience I had of losing someone and I did feel very sad. But then I thought about the fact that she had had a very long and enjoyable life, apart from the last few years, because she suffered from dementia, but she had had a very enjoyable life, so I think it's the memories we hang onto and associate with.

From this unbidden memory, Isaac constructs a positive story of his Grandmother, the memories he has of her and the benefits these bring him.

Recollections of loved ones illustrated through material objects, whether selected purposefully or stumbled upon during everyday life, made a significant contribution to the exploration of death, dying and memorialisation for these young–people. As the lids were taken off the boxes it was clear that many contained items of remembrance, which evoked strong feelings and emotional responses. Hallam and Hockey (2001) comment that we often choose to communicate our memories to others via stories and/or photographs, and that this promotes a feeling of agency or control over our recollections, remembrances and reminiscences of those we knew and loved. The young-people, I believe, demonstrated their agency in choosing, showing and sharing the objects contained in the boxes and the feelings associated with them. They negotiated the 'emotional power' (Sontag 2003: 107) of the items within the context of opportunity and friendship. The variety and number of artefacts was quite astonishing and the array of objects illustrated the importance of these often-mundane everyday items alongside the precious keepsakes, as mementoes. The sharing of stories, stuff and emotions, as commented on by Valentine, 'conveyed the extent to which they were engaged in preserving and affirming the unique personhood and continuing social significance of deceased loved ones and their relationship with them' (2008: 172).

Gillis argues that the 'dead sustain the living' (1997: 221) and this would appear to be so within the everyday objects that fill our homes and remind us of the lives of friends, relatives, and pets. The objects brought to the conversation groups, such as Ruth's blue ceramic dolphin, plus the photographs and ephemera discussed within this section demonstrate how emotional connections with the dead are retained and maintained. Will's poetry for his Grandma expressed how feelings for those we have loved and continue to do so, are made apparent; and Jo's photograph exhibited our continuing bonds with the dead. The words of Thomas Baldwin Thayer (1864) were used by Gillis to express these ideas,

> In every home there is an enshrined memory, a scared relic, a ring, a lock of shining hair, a broken plaything, a book, something sacredly kept and guarded, which speaks of death, which tells us as plainly as words, of someone long since gone (1997: 211)

To complete this section and reflect upon the emotional meaning of all this 'stuff' to these young-people, I would like to describe a particularly interesting incident. John (aged 15) brings his Grandfather's ashes to the discussion group.

John: Well I've brought my Granddad's ashes [he produces a brown plastic container, and places it on the table, everyone around the table looks at the container]. He died like a couple of months ago, yeah, on Dec 21st he died, and I just thought it was appropriate to bring him today. [John unscrews the lid and peers inside; he then directs the opened container to the other boys around the table]. Do you want to put your hand in? [Boys start to stand up in order to look and perhaps feel inside].

This was a recent and significant death to John. He proudly presents his Grandfather's ashes, accompanied by the death certificate, to the group. As if the brown plastic container with a white label bearing his Grandfather's name is not enough to demonstrate the reality of this death, John removes the lid and invites us to peer inside at the remains, which receives an enthusiastic response. Having seen the ashes John suggests that the other boys might like to put their hands in and touch them. A second or two of uncertainty and hesitancy followed ... and it was in that moment, the one and only instant during any of these conversations, that I stepped in; asking the boys if they felt this was a 'good idea'. They took a second to think, sat back down and John replaced the lid. On reflection, I still wonder why I did this. Having encouraged these young-people to metaphorically lift the lid on death and peer inside, why did I stop at touching it? My response, I know, was prompted by visions of spilt ashes, vacuum cleaners and unhappy parents.

Virtual Memories for Sharing: Death on-Line

Veale (2004) highlights how recent changes in Western society have had an impact on forms of memorialisation. For example, the use of solid memorials, such as headstones, are becoming outmoded, due in part to the need of the bereaved to pay physical visits to the cemetery or graveyard, which may be geographically problematic when relatives live some distance away. Therefore, the need for an alternative space is identified. This chapter identifies that young-people have, alongside many adults, found and adopted an alternate space for the sharing of death related ideas and memories; cyberspace. Livingstone comments that the young have been dubbed the 'digital generation' (2009: 1), due to their expertise with new technologies. Perhaps, it is these particular skills that have drawn them so readily to the internet as a source of death related knowledge and participation. Caroll and Landry (2010) note that what was once seen as the sole preserve of religious ceremonies, gravesites and funeral homes has more recently become the remit of on-line spaces. In particular, they point to the ready use of on-line social networks by young-people to grieve and memorialise, questioning how this is changing the norms of what is socially and culturally acceptable. The following accounts feature the knowledge and understanding that these young-people demonstrate in relation to web based memorial sites. It reports their diverse and changing views about the relevance and benefits of these to both themselves and to families of the dead. Similarly, online blogs and in particular the website PostSecrets is show-cased as a space in which ideas about death can be shared without fear of judgement or censorship.

The recent death of a boy at school prompted the following, in which a group of 15-year-old girls discuss how people are remembered on Facebook by leaving virtual flowers, hearts and short messages.

Sally: On Facebook they were saying things like, 'I don't even know you but I'm so sorry'.

Ellie: Yeah, like RIP. On Facebook I've got so many flowers.

SC: Sorry, what do you mean?

Sally: It's like, well someone on MSN [Microsoft messaging service] asked everyone to put a flower in front of your name in memory of [name]

Ellie: Yes, after he died, this person said can everyone put a flower in front of their name, but it in no way expresses the way you are feeling. But I did do it and then took it off after a week because I thought it should be a limited time.

Sally: There's still loads of flowers around.

Megan: It's cos like when anyone dies, it's the way people react to it through MSN and the media, and they put flowers and hearts there.

Sally: And like within a day that he died 500 people had joined his Facebook

Ellie: It's because [teacher's name] did that fantastic speech about how good he was. It makes you think about how you want to be remembered, and if people would put in any bad stuff about you, cos people do write bad stuff. But, they usually find something, your best qualities and hype them up, which is quite nice.

Carroll and Landry name these 'virtual black armbands' (2010: 345), which identify the poster as someone who is part of and shares with the grief of others. The girls acknowledge the popularity of this type of memorialisation but question its ability to fully express their feelings.

The following group, also of a similar age, Laura, Jack and Amy, demonstrate their emerging attitudes to the use of online social networks as sites of grief and remembrance. Jack initially shares his thoughts that an actual bunch of flowers would mean more to a grieving family than a post on Facebook but latterly proposes that an online comment might also be helpful. Both groups of young-people express a degree of pressure from their peers to conform to requests to post visible symbols of grief, which they question. In particular, they consider what length of time is appropriate to leave the symbols and the importance of having a relationship with the dead person and not just jumping on the bandwagon as they see it. Equally, the explore the retribution that follows if you do not obey the rules, and the authenticity of some of the comments.

Jack: You can put things on Facebook and stuff like that, but I personally think that's not good because if you had really cared about someone you could take a bunch of flowers round to the family, and I think that would mean much more.

Laura: Like if someone sends you a little comment on MSN saying to remember so-and-so, like the baby who died in the news the other day then I don't want to do that because I don't feel connected to him, and although it's very sad, it's slightly pointless.

Amy: Yes, like when Madeleine McCann went missing everyone put flowers on and everything, and like I care about it in a distant way because it's not very nice but I don't really know them.

Laura: And like on MSN, the family isn't going to see it only your friends so it has no meaning.

Amy: Also there's a peer pressure thing when everyone says 'have you put flowers on' and stuff, and then say 'I hate you' if you haven't. So I think people get carried away a bit. Although when I left [she mentions name of previous school] they put a Bebo page saying they were going to miss me, and people were signing saying they were going to miss me, and if I died it would be quite cool to have a page where people would write nice things about me. I think it's quite nice.

Jack: I think it would be good for the family, it would mean a lot to them I think, that people would still think about them.

Laura: But what if nobody left a comment? That would be hard and depressing. [Thoughtful silence]. I suppose it can be good because you can set up stuff like web sites, that you can always remember people on, like you just log onto that and remember them. And there are other sites that you can send money to, to help people who are dying or so that you can donate blood and stuff like that.

The use of social networking sites as a space for memorials is accepted by young- people as a way of expressing solidarity and sharing their feelings in the face of death. That these spaces are popular with the young is understandable but that the pressure to participate in ways that are seen as 'correct' and is as strongly policed as any traditional family funeral, is perhaps quite a surprise. Carroll and Landry observe that despite the general understanding that spaces such as Facebook can provide an open and non-judgemental arena to express feelings there is 'similarly, lurking, a surveillance phenomenon or practice that is common online' (2010: 348). Likewise, Woodthorpe, in her discussion of memorialisation in contemporary cemeteries, observes 'powerful normalising discourses' (2010: 131), which judge what is deemed to be appropriate/

inappropriate memorial activity. The young-people's responses, seem to suggest that the same can be said of online memorials.

Two further online sources were acknowledged as spaces in which these young-people felt they could encounter death, remember friends and relatives, express their feelings and explore the ideas of others. These were, online blogs and in particular the site 'PostSecret'; described on its web-page, as 'an ongoing community art project where people e-mail their secrets anonymously on one side of a homemade postcard' (PostSecret 2013). First, a group of 17 year olds briefly discuss their use of blogs relating to death.

> **Paul**: Now with blogs and stuff, I get quite a few blogs on death and what people think on things like Facebook, and people discuss it quite openly because on the internet you are anonymous and you are free to say what you like. Like on blogspot.com you can talk about anything. No one knows who you are, or where you live, so no one can come and batter you. So blogs are so much easier to communicate on.
>
> **Claire**: Yeah, you can say what you think
>
> **Mike**: Yeah, you can't get your face smashed in for saying the wrong thing.

Similarly, a group of 15-year-olds discuss their use of the PostSecret site, on which they suggest they and others can share thoughts and feelings about death and the memories of loved ones, good or bad, without censure. They compare actual objects as forms of memorialisation with virtual methods of remembering. This lengthy discussion demonstrates the importance of this site to these particular girls and uncovers some interesting points in relation to alternative forms of remembering and their freedom to express ideas in a more expansive way.

> **Jo**: The other thing I've got is a PostSecrets book and this one is *Confessions on Life, Death and God.*
>
> **SC**: Ok, what's a PostSecrets book?
>
> **Lucy**: Shall I explain this?

Jo Yes, go on then.

Lucy: I discovered this while looking at random things on the internet. It's a site by Frank Warren, and when he was starting out he asked people to send him a postcard confessing their secrets, and now it's just grown and grown and grown and thousands of people send in secrets. Some are quite simple like 'I don't always wash my hand after going to the toilet', and others are like 'everyone who knew me before 9/11 thinks I'm dead'. And he puts them on his web site, about 20 each Sunday, and they're called Sunday Secrets. They can have artwork on them and they can be really deep secrets.

Jo: I mean there's one in here that just says 'call me, Dad died'. I mean you just read through them on Sunday and think how awful things are for some people.

SC: But why do you post?

Lucy: I think it's the relief of sending one. I mean I've written some and they haven't been published, but it's the fact that you send them. You send it to someone who's not going to judge you, they don't know you. It's not like you're saying it to a friend who could spill it to someone. They don't know who you are.

Jo: Yeah, I think it's because no one knows who you are. You can say absolutely anything about anything, even death and sadness and losing someone. I mean you can send a postcard about death and no one's going to think you're a sad morbid creature who thinks about nothing but death and stuff.

Helen: I think it's like just as important as having some of the objects we showed that reminded us of people, because like it's sometimes easier to write things down than say things in words. Cos it gets you used to the idea that someone is dead rather than just having something there.

Lucy: Yeah, I think it's both. I think it helps because you can express yourself and let go. It's a way of letting go and having objects is a way of holding on, and we do both with the relationships we had, both letting go and holding on.

SC: So do you think you should hold on to the relationships after someone is dead?

Helen: Well I don't think you should forget them because they have added to all the experiences in your life and made you who you are. So if you forget that you are forgetting part of yourself in a way. You need to let go of them enough so that you're not sad all the time because you still have to live your life

Jo: Yeah, I think like PostSecrets and stuff are like new ways of dealing with death. One of the secrets says, 'I hope when I die it's with a machete in one hand, a sword in the other, and taking down as many zombies as I can'. It sort-of takes a comical look at death and that helps I think because people are frightened of death. I like this one too, it's like on an envelope and it says, 'Before I go on a trip I write a letter to my family in case I die'. I think that's really sweet and really sad.

Helen: It's nice reading them because you get to see other people's ideas about death.

Jo: Just got to finish on this one, 'There better be sex in heaven'. [All laugh].

PostSecret is clearly significant to this group of girls. They use the space to express personal feelings and share in those of others. For them the total anonymity and lack of judgment makes this site important and relevant. They articulate a 'sense of relief', even if their post is not published, at being able to air their views, however strange, without the disapproval of others. They use PostSecret to express and acknowledge diverse perspectives, which although unsaid, may be considered by them to be unacceptable topics of conversation to have with adults. For example, death that explores comical, unusual or sexual connotations. Death in a myriad of guises is up for grabs within the pages of PostSecret and provides space for exploration and reflection. Lucy suggests the site provides the opportunity to both 'let go' and 'hold onto' relationships with the dead. Helen believes that both of these are necessary, as by completely letting go you let go of part of yourself but you have to let go enough to be able to live your own life. For these girls this website provided a virtual 'kitchen table', around which any aspect of death and dying could be displayed, alongside the valuable and insightful connections made with the feelings and ideas of others. Resulting in 'you can say anything about anything, even death'.

The use of social networking sites, blogs and web pages as online communities in which young-people can share in memorialisation and death related issues is becoming commonplace. De Vries and Rutherford suggest that 'memorializing on the World Wide Web is a new phenomenon offering significant potential for the creation of new postdeath rituals' (2004: 18). These young-people know where death, in many different forms, is to be found on the Internet. They occupy these spaces largely uninterrupted, sharing their thoughts and ideas without fear of recrimination. However, expectations and conflicting views from peers concerning appropriate postings, length of mourning and who should participate were evident and uncovered that, as with other memorial sites, conflict was present. Just as Woodthorpe describes the contemporary cemetery as 'a dynamic space filled with assumptions, activities and perspectives, some of which are contradictory', and goes on to comment that it provides a 'space in which private emotion (grief) and public behaviour (mourning) intersect in potentially problematic ways' (2010: 117), so too is the contemporary virtual cemetery, the internet. As young-people continue to use these spaces in order to remember dead friends and relatives, chat with others, share ideas and feelings, they may set out new roles and rules for exploring and sharing in death as part of everyday life. O'Neill (2008) declares that the memory of the dead has passed into our control. However, for these young-people and for those of the future the internet may successfully fill the hushed lacuna of adult deathspace for them. I wonder, are adults willing to let this pass out of their control?

Deaths for Staging: Songs, Souls and Science Fiction

The three previous sections have outlined young-people's unique and personal encounters with death. Stories have been told of the deaths of loved relatives and friends, meaningful objects have provided lasting memories and demonstrated their impact on the living, and more recent forms of memorialisation available on the internet have been explored and shared. Although the close proximity of these accounts, to the young-people, cannot be denied and furthermore their rich connectedness to actual and virtual networks relating to mortality, the intimate consideration of their own end-of-life rituals and their positive evaluation of these came as a surprise.

Chronological age typically positions the young at a comfortable distance from the end-of-life. Therefore, a willingness to visualise and review personal death, might demonstrate a certain removal from or possible idealisation of death. However, I suggest various conversations, situated throughout this book, and in particular the ones about to be considered now, potentially contest this. Until this point, death has been viewed as 'other than self', however close or distant that other may be. In the following conversations death is now very much represented by the 'self' and the staging, rehearsing and planning of 'my' death and death rituals. Death, in this way, is brought yet another step closer and acknowledges a reciprocal relationship.

Across all the age groups, possibilities for the individual's body after death, arose. For example, Amy (aged 15) mentions her wish to be an organ donor.

> **Amy**: I've told my parents that if I die before they do then I want them to donate all my organs and stuff to save someone else.

> Justine (aged 11) examines the possibility of being frozen and brought back to life in the future.

> **Justine**: They've got this thing about how you can freeze your body and bring you back to life in the future [hesitates]. I might quite like that.

> On a separate occasion, Charlotte (aged 15) evaluates her own reasons for not wanting this.

> **Charlotte**: The frozen thing, um, you can be frozen but why would you want to be unfrozen. If I were frozen and then unfrozen, when I came back I'd have no friends and I'd be lonely and I'd be so confused. It's like people in prison when they come out they can't fit in with society.

> Megan (aged 15) talks about the possibility of being made into a necklace, an idea that Charlie (aged 10) also considers.

Megan: Do you know you can be made into a jewel like a diamond, I think I'd quite like that. I could be made into a necklace and generations of people could wear me.

Charlie: Or you could put your ashes in a pendant and people could remember you in that way.

Tom and Lottie (both aged 10) consider the possibility of 'special boxes'.

Tom: I want to be remembered when I'm dead, because like when I die I want my body to be burned and put like in a special box or something. Then when my Great-Great-Great Grandchildren come along and say 'Daddy what's this', they can say who it is and remember me like that.

Lottie: Or you could have a box and put all your favourite things in it, and paint it purple, that's my favourite colour, and put photographs in it and things, and people could look through it and know who you were.

The ideas presented above represent a blurring of the previously clear boundaries between life and death and link to a continuation of person-hood into the future. For example, discussions that centre around organ donation, bodies being frozen and being brought back to life, transformation into a necklace a traditional form of keepsake, or being put in a box and remembered by future generations, suggest a persistence of self. The person, in this way, continues to exist or be present even after death, often disguised in another form. Equally pertinent, is the developing response to death and loss, which has led these young-people to engage in their own mortality. Death, previously viewed at a distance has gradually edged its way forward and merged with the self. Aspects of Miller and Parrott's anthropological discussion on loss and material culture in London seems pertinent at this point, as they argue for our gradual 'divestment and separation' (2009: 516) from those we love, via their material belongings. However, notwithstanding this slow and gentle disassociation from death, I feel the young-people here have rather performed a rapid association with and investment in death, as they move towards performing, staging and rehearsing their own end-of-life scenarios. The enactment of these rituals establishes impermanence as part of themselves.

The following exchanges showcase some of the ideas young-people have about their own end-of-life ceremonies and how they would like to be remembered. Lucy (aged 15) begins by considering two contrasting types of behaviour, which she has seen and are often prevalent at end-of-life rituals, those of crying and being stoical.

> **Lucy**: I've got another picture of an old person and someone crying cos this is the vision you always have of mothers on television screaming and crying for their children who have died, and when I die I do actually want people to cry over me. Some people would say 'oh I don't want people to cry over me', but I want people to cry because it shows that they loved me and care that I have gone. Or I suppose some people might be happy.
>
> **Jo** (aged 15): I won't be happy when you die. That would be awful. God!

Crying, Lucy feels, is appropriate, if people cry at her funeral it will show that people loved and cared for her. Alternatively, another group of 15-year-old girls consider the traditional custom of wearing black.

> **Sally**: I think at my funeral I wouldn't want people to wear black, I would want it to be more-happy I think.
>
> **Ellie**: I wouldn't want people to wear black and mourn me leaving. I'd want them to celebrate the fact that I'd been in their life. Today at school we talked about death; we talked about what songs we wanted playing at our funeral. I said I wanted, 'Bye bye baby, baby bye bye', by the Bay City Rollers, or 'I've had the time of my life' from Dirty Dancing, or 'Bye bye my lover' by James Blunt. [All laugh and start to sing].

Both Sally and Ellie suggest that they would want their funerals to be cheerful occasions where life is celebrated rather than mourned. Ellie mentions a number of songs with amusing and pertinent titles that she would like playing. Charlie also subscribes to the idea of a cheerful end-of-life ritual by suggesting,

> **Charlie** (aged 10): I know that at my funeral I don't really want people to sit in a dark room and watch me burn. I want them to have a good time, and have like a disco or something.

Ellie and Charlotte move on to discuss what Ellie terms the 'key thing', which is to be buried or cremated. She terms this in stark language as being 'eaten or burnt'.

Ellie: The key thing is though; do you want to be eaten by worms or do you want to be burnt?

Charlotte: I think I want to be cremated, but I don't think I want even the teeniest, teeniest, teeniest bit of my ash to get away because that's part of me, so I want to be kept together.

Ellie: Perhaps I could get part of me cremated and part of me buried. [All: No No!!!!]. Then I could get half of me buried and get a grave stone, and part of me ashes, and then I could have the whole lot. [All: Laugh]

Contrasting views arise here, in which Charlotte suggests she would prefer to be cremated but that her body must very definitely be kept together. Even the smallest amount of her body escaping from the ashes might mean she is no longer whole and this seems to concern her. In response Ellie shows no qualms about her body after life, indicating that she could be both cremated and buried, thereby having the best of everything. This does not appear a popular approach amongst her peers. Continuing this theme Lucy also reflects on the idea of her ashes being placed in a plastic bag.

Lucy: I have also got a picture of someone sprinkling ashes. I thought it was quite a symbolic thing and that it might be nice to sprinkle my ashes everywhere but then they've got them in a plastic bag, and I thought that's not so nice. I don't want my body in a plastic bag or anyone else's body in a plastic bag because that's like their whole soul and their whole life and you don't want to be throwing it away. I want to be buried or cremated and not put in a plastic bag.

Lucy associates the plastic bag with being thrown away. She equates this with throwing away someone's whole life and their soul, and therefore inappropriate. Laura feels that the best thing to do is to make your own choice and not stick with traditional views and practices.

> **Laura** (aged 15): One of our friends died and she wasn't a relative or any-thing but she wanted everyone to be happy and have a good time.
>
> **SC**: Do you think that was good?
>
> **Laura**: I think it's good to interpret things how you want them to be and not just go with tradition, so you can make your own choice. I want to make my own choice.

Laura demonstrates her agency here by considering the choices she will make about her own death. She does not at this point say what they will be, but that she wants to make those choices herself. She demonstrates awareness of her own death and the possibility of a ritual to dispose of her body. She however, will make a choice that best portrays her views on life and death and not strictly adhere to those of tradition.

Although none of these young-people were in the narrowest sense of the word dying, Seale's evaluation of the experience of dying in con-temporary Western seems apt. He suggests that the combination of the 'dying role' and new forms of heroic cultural scripts develop an 'open awareness' of dying, as discussed previously. This mixture, he continues, 'imbue[s] the experience with meaning', thus giving dying people 'the opportunity to become mourners, presiding over their own mortuary rites and participating in the construction of an imagined caring com-munity' (1998: 119). Living with the full awareness that their lives are ephemeral, these young-people can assume and extend the dying role to themselves and stage the possibilities of their own deaths, not only for themselves, but for the people around them.

Conclusion

In drawing together, the many ideas represented in this chapter it seems clear that narratives, photographs, objects and online forums all pro-vide opportunities for letting death out of the box, however briefly. Equally, the creation of space and time to allow for these conversations to occur generated moments in which the end-of-life could be shared and showed, staged and storied and embellished with humour and performance, tears and reflection, silence and noise. Poignant moments were cherished and humorous ones welcomed.

Death, as demonstrated here, is encountered in the lives of young-people in numerous forms, and this chapter has allowed us to share in a variety of experiences, responses and personal stories. Modes of death and reactions to it were not constant, uniform or lacklustre but disparate, assorted and vital and this must surely encourage further exploration of young-people's ideas. Popular constructions of childhood, as considered earlier, situate the younger child as innocent and those slightly older as possibly indifferent, both as resources for the future, and death as having no part to play in this stage of their lives. However, I believe the accounts, represented here, question and challenge such views. Within these conversations young-people have shown concern, involvement and agency, not detachment, indifference and powerlessness. Life and death are experienced and encountered by them as 'beings', existing in the here and now, and not something that can be put off until societal views deem the time appropriate to reveal the 'mysteries' of it to them.

Deaths and stories, memories and experiences, have been showcased in a myriad of different ways and through a multiplicity of items. The stories and experiences of these young-people are vibrant, often amusing, sometimes angry and frequently sad. The deaths they shared with each other, and now with us, exhibit their participation in traditional and more contemporary approaches to death, the impact of death on their everyday lives and their dedication to the perpetuation of personhood and continuing bonds with loved friends and family. In staging end-of-life rituals, death becomes incorporated into the self-concept, and personal philosophies and ideas of what death is and what lies beyond the death of the self is the content of the next chapter.

Once the lids were lifted from these boxes and the importance of the dead within them freed, layer upon layer of invisible other boxes were opened, one inside another like a nest of Russian dolls. These layers illuminated the complexity, diversity, and multiplicity of approaches that young-people have on this topic. It is impossible to gather these ideas into one box and attest that this is the way all young-people think about, memorialise and react to the deaths of significant others. However, it is possible to say that providing a space to encounter ideas enables many versions of death and dying to be explored in a non-judgmental atmosphere, and highlights how other young-people may respond, react and engage with death in creative, vibrant and imaginative ways. Once the box is opened we cannot close the lid; what young-people appear to be waiting for are more opportunities to peer inside.

References

Carroll, B., & Landry, K. (2010). Logging on and letting out: Using social networks to Grieve and to Mourn. *Bulletin of Science, Technology & Society, 30*(5), 341–349.

De Vries, B., & Rutherford, J. (2004). Memorializing loved ones on the world wide web. *Omega—Journal of Death and Dying, 49*(1), 5–26.

Frank, A. W. (2010). *Letting stories breathe: A socio-narratology.* Chicago: The University of Chicago Press.

Gibson, M. (2004). Melancholy objects. *Mortality, 9*(4), 285–299.

Gillis, J. R. (1997). *A world of their own making: Myth, ritual, and the quest for family values.* Massachusetts: Harvard University Press.

Hallam, E., & Hockey, J. (2001). *Death, Memory and material culture.* Oxford: Berg.

Hockey, J., Komaromy, C., & Woodthorpe, K. (2010). Materialising absence. In J. Hockey, C. Komaromy, & K. Woodthorpe (Eds.), *The matter of death: Space, place and materiality.* Palgrave MacMillan: Basingstoke.

Howarth, G. (2007). *Death and dying: A sociological introduction.* Cambridge: Polity Press.

Kaufman, K. R., & Kaufman, N. D. (2006). And then the dog died. *Death Studies, 30,* 61–76.

Livingstone, S. (2009). *Children and the internet.* Cambridge: Polity Press.

Machin, L. (2009). *Working with loss and grief: A new model for practitioners.* London: Sage.

Miller, D., & Parrott, F. (2009). Loss and material culture in South London. *Journal of the Royal Anthropological Institute, 15,* 502–519.

O'Neill, K. D. (2008). Death. *Lives, and Video Streams, Mortality, 13*(2), 174–186.

Pollock, D. (1990). Telling the told: Performing like a family. *Oral History Review, 18*(2), 1–36.

PostSecret. (2013). http://www.postsecret.com. Accessed April 1 2012.

Salinger, J. D. (1951). *The Catcher in the Rye.* London: Penguin.

Seale, C. (1998). *Constructing death: The sociology of dying and bereavement.* Cambridge: Cambridge University Press.

Sontag, S. (2003). *Regarding the pain of others.* London: Penguin.

Timmermans, S. (2005). Death brokering: Constructing culturally appropriate deaths. *Sociology of Health & Illness, 27*(7), 993–1013.

Valentine, C. (2006). Academic constructions of bereavement. *Mortality, 11*(1), 57–78.

Valentine, C. (2008). *Bereavement narratives: Continuing bonds in the twenty-first century.* London: Routledge.

Veale, K. (2004). Online memorialisation: The web as a collective memorial landscape for remembering the dead. *The Fibreculture Journal, 3.* http://three. fibreculturejournal.org/fcj-014-online-memorialisation-the-web-as-a-collective-memorial-landscape-for-remembering-the-dead/. Accessed July 28 2011.

Woodthorpe, K. (2010). Private grief in public spaces: Interpreting memorialisation in the contemporary cemetery. In J. Hockey, C. Komaromy, & K. Woodthorpe (Eds.), *The matter of death: Space.* Place and Materiality, Basingstoke: Palgrave Macmillan.

5

'We're All Made of Dead People'

Introduction

The two previous chapter have explored young-peoples' everyday experiences of and encounters with death through the media, death at a distance, and subsequently through personal experience, death up-close. This chapter takes another direction, investigating their personal and highly distinctive 'deathscapes'. These are everyday intrapersonal spaces in which death can be reflected upon, questioned and interrogated, death as philosophy. Maddrell and Sidaway (2010) use the term 'deathscape' to highlight the importance of geographical place and space to our understanding of death. I use the term here to refer to an inner world, an often hidden landscape, in which young-people search for meaning and understanding in the face of mortality. The following conversations are an invitation into previously 'undiscovered countries' where fragmentary perceptions, ideas, beliefs, values and attitudes are briefly glimpsed. They provide an ever changing and shifting kaleidoscope of thoughts, and can be exciting and unusual places to visit.

© The Author(s) 2017
S. Coombs, *Young People's Perspectives on End-of-Life*,
Studies in Childhood and Youth, DOI 10.1007/978-3-319-53631-6_5

Whilst Seale comments that life can sometimes be understood as 'a deliberate, continual turning away from death' (1998: 11), these young-people, on the contrary, confront and explore such issues head-on. Whilst they readily acknowledge 'truths', such as the universalism and inevitability of death and the fears these can engender, they in the words of Wall 'open[ed] the mind to creative new horizons' (2010: 176). They create a meaningful world in a life that ultimately leads to death by drawing upon an array of creative, imaginative, dynamic and open-minded resources. Wall suggests that,

> As life develops, everyone on some level must struggle to come to terms with their own death. But this struggle is part of a larger struggle, experienced just as profoundly by children and adults alike, to come to terms with having been born into time as a new and particular interpreter of time (2010: 66).

We shall see, throughout this chapter, how these young-people negotiate their everyday ideas of earthly time and finitude.

The Inevitability of Death

That death is an inevitable, inescapable and an everyday part of human existence is clearly accepted by these young-people. However, whilst emphasising the expected nature of it, they also identify attempts by adults to hide death from them. They suggest that death, as a topic of conversation, is often side-stepped and feared by adults and perhaps also by the young. The inevitability of death is viewed as beyond their control but something that links humanity together.

Young-people from across the age-range confronted and accepted the reality of death, as John (aged 15) points out 'you live and you die and that's it'. Milly and Charlotte separately concur.

> **Milly** (aged 10): You can't die unless you have been alive. No one can die without being alive first. So, it's like you can't have one without the other.

Charlotte (aged 15): To be fair though everybody's going to die.

These statements are clear, logical and decisive: death is indeed going to happen to everyone and is 'just part of life'. However, complications with this clarity soon arise, death cannot be viewed quite so dispassionately. Megan and Ellie, both aged 15, whilst demonstrating their understanding of the inevitability of mortality, suggest a tendency to hide from its stark reality, an ability to 'lie' in order to conceal the devastation of losing someone significant. As Howells suggests 'it is love that makes us fear death, love of self, and love of the other: we fear losing our very selves when we risk losing what we love' (2011: 2–3).

> **Megan:** All people die, and it's a lie in some sense, but we tend to think that we're not going to lose anyone significant until we're a lot older, but you do. There are lots of people around who have lost someone.
>
> **Ellie:** It's [thinking that close relatives and friends are not going to die] like a fluffy cushion that's going to make everything better.

Megan questions 'the lie', the attempt to put death out of sight, by acknowledging the undeniable truth that many people, one or two perhaps known to her, have indeed suffered the loss of close friends or relatives. Ellie uses the imagery of a 'fluffy cushion' as a metaphorical means to hide from the experience of losing those close to her, and yet her response indicates her ability to meet head-on the fact that this, and indeed no other object, can protect her from this harsh reality.

Isaac (aged 15) continues this theme of avoidance by considering societal attempts to oppose the inevitability of death by scientific treatments. He refers to this as the 'culture around death', linking it to what he sees as an overarching steering-clear-of and fear of death by society. As Becker suggests 'of all things that move man, one of the principal ones is his terror of death' (1973: 11).

> **Isaac:** I was reading about this scientist who was trying to tackle what he called the seven or eight deadly things about life, and he proposed a treatment that you go in for about the age of 50 or something, and it takes about 30 years off your life or something [in the way you look]. It's weird; well I think it's weird, the culture around death. Well it seems that people are so scared about death that they are trying to avoid it perpetually, which I find personally really creepy

Isaac suggests that trying to avoid death, in a broad sense, and also in relation to more specific and scientific attempts to prevent aging and extend life is 'weird' and 'creepy'. Similarly, he goes on to explain how fear and evasion of death, often by adults, leads them to steer-clear of the topic and thereby miss the opportunity to discuss and confront issues of mortality with children and young-people.

> **Isaac:** I think young children are suppressed from talking about death or don't have death explained to them as well as it could be, because adults are afraid of it.
>
> **SC:** Why?
>
> **Isaac:** I think to protect children. I think a lot of it goes on. I've asked lots of people to join in with these interviews and talk about death who could not get parental consent to do so but seemed quite enthusiastic to do so, which is a shame. I do think young-people are protected from it to a certain extent. I mean it would be damaging to just tell a three-year-old that one day you are going to die. I don't think that would be particularly positive [Pauses. Group affirms this by nodding in agreement].
>
> **Andrew** (aged 16): No but explaining what does happen is [positive] and children can accept that.

Isaac and Andrew consider the undeveloped potential of young-people to engage in this topic, and lay the blame firmly at the foot of adult protectionism. They assert that young children can and do 'accept' the inevitable nature of death and that discussing it with them would be a positive move. Similarly, Berridge identifies the censorship of death by adults and society as an 'anomaly' a 'glaring omission'. She points to a 'disparity' between children's actual exposure to death, in ways already discussed in previous chapters, and what she terms a 'a cultural conspiracy to conceal real death' (2002: 6).

Claire (aged 17) takes a rounded view, both supporting Isaac's stance that death should be talked about more, whilst equally incorporating Megan and Ellie's ideas that people are scared of dying and therefore try to avoid the topic. She introduces death as 'controversial' despite its inevitability, reflecting on this approach as 'silly'.

> **Claire**: It's not talked about, well it is talked about but it's still controversial. I know it sounds really silly because everyone dies but it's like something you avoid talking about, isn't it? It's not really like something so simple that you could just mention it or drop it into a conversation and just talk about it. I think we should talk about and think about it but people are scared, people are scared of dying. (Pauses).

> **Mike** (age 17): I know you might not want to think about it but it's the circle of life, one person dies and one is born and that's it.

> **Claire**: It's part of life.

Ultimately Claire and Mike return to the well-trodden paths of earlier discussions; the inevitability of death as part of life. Seale's contention that 'social and cultural life involves turning away from the inevitability of death […] and towards life' (1998:1) seems pertinent once again. Arguably, it is possible to suggest that in these discussions, prior to focusing on life, the young-people considered, confronted and reflected upon death first. That they can and do reflect upon and explore the concept of death, both pertaining to themselves and to a wider society, is not surprising. However, the ways in which they juggle multiple ideas, both balancing, questioning and exploring alternating concepts of acceptance, fear, avoidance, protectionism and inevitability highlights the complexity of their ideas and illustrates the rich and colourful landscapes of death they encounter. Sometimes these landscapes are unsettling places, as we shall see next.

In contrast to some of the more inclusive and overarching reflections on the inevitability of death, we now turn to an individual deathscape. Ellie (aged 15) expresses her own deep fears of death and dying, in which she confronts her images of dying young, dying suddenly, dying in hospital and dying whilst travelling.

Ellie: I have a picture of a very, very old lady being kissed by a very young lady, because whenever I think of death I think of old people. I don't like to think of young-people dying, because I like to imagine that people who die are either very frail or they're very old, so that it isn't so much of a shock. If I think of someone being hit by a bus, I tell myself they had a terminal illness and that they would have died anyway so that I don't feel so bad about the fact that they died.

Charlotte (aged 15): To be fair though everybody's going to die.

Ellie: Yeah I know, but it's easier for me if I think of them as old. I have a picture of a hospital and a hospital bed because when I think of hospitals, death sort of comes into my mind, and if I'm told I have to spend a night in hospital then I immediately think it's really serious and I'm going to die. I worry about everything; I worry about getting on public transport that I'm going to die.

Continuing, she suggests that her nightmares, crying and not being able to sleep lead her to believe she has a phobia about death. However, the exploration of these ideas, with the support of her friends, allows her to reflect upon and examine what she is afraid of.

Ellie: I had really bad nightmares about dying. I used not to be able to sleep because …. [trails off]. I forgot, but I do really have a phobia about death. If I think about it, it makes me cry. It's not, it's not the dying or leaving anyone else behind, it's the not knowing what happens when you die.

Ellie's worries are centred on 'not knowing'. She accepts she will die; she knows she will leave loved ones behind but her journey takes her beyond the well-trodden paths of some of her friends to less certain territory.

Whilst accepting the universality of death, it is evident that young-people also recognise, question and reflect upon the so-called 'lies', the fears and the avoidance present in broader societal views. Isaac raised the issue of adult anxiety, trepidation and protectionism and Claire agreed that fear is a big factor in discussing end-of-life issues. In a similar way, Helen and Amy (aged 15), consider why people prefer not to think about death, and conclude that concentrating on life is more important.

Helen: I don't think people want to think about death or what happens after it or doesn't. I think they push it to the back of their minds so they can concentrate on life.

Amy: Death is like, well you don't know when it's going to come and you can't prepare for it so you need to be ready for it whenever, but if you spent your whole time worrying about it you wouldn't really be living so you need to be aware of it, but not dwell on it all the time.

Both Helen and Amy take the view that people do not want to think about death and therefore they push it away, so that life and living pre-occupy human thoughts rather than death and dying. Amy confronts the lack of control that humans have over their own deaths, yet despite its everyday nature and regular occurrence, she considers that constantly thinking about it would constitute 'not living'.

Lucy (aged 15) extends this idea of humanities lack of control over death and dying by applying the idea to herself. She describes how she can command both life and death within her computer game but regretfully concedes that she cannot do this in 'real life'.

Lucy: Well, I've brought 'The Sims' [brings computer game out of box] because I like The Sims, but also if they don't like what I want them to do I put them in the swimming pool and remove the steps so they can't get out and then they die. Or, if they're not doing well in school because they've got a boyfriend and don't do their homework, or they're always moaning because they're tired because I'm trying to make them into geniuses I get very annoyed and lock them in a room and eventually the grim reaper comes and zaps them and they die. It's very sad but less trouble for me. You see I sometimes get carried away when I'm making the families and they have like three babies and three teenagers so there are too many demands, so I get fed up and kill one off. It's strange, I know it's a warped view of life, a bit twisted. I just... I like to control things and I can in this game but not in real life.

Notwithstanding such entertaining and humorous insights into a virtual world, Lucy's inner deathscape reveals more challenging terrain, over which she has no jurisdiction. She finds this lack of control over actual death difficult to contemplate.

This section began by focusing on what might, at first, appear to be a tacit acceptance of the inevitability of death. However, pragmatic and realistic deathscapes soon gave way to a concerned lack of control, death is not something that can be hidden from, and equally in order to get on with one's life, not something to dwell on too often either. A number of questions were also raised: If death is a usual part of everyday life why do we try to hide from it? Why do adults try and protect us from it? Why do people go to extraordinary lengths to try and avoid it? Why do we try and control it? Just as death is inescapable these reflections unavoidably raised more questions than answers. Finally, Jack and Amy bring the questions to a close, stating their belief in death as the single unifier of humanity. I will let their eloquent words and original description (via the use of an everyday household object) bring this section to a close.

> **Amy** (aged 15): Finally, I brought a USB cable, I'm not sure why, but something about death connecting everybody and different kinds of people because they have different ends [she holds up cable to demonstrate the different types of end]. I don't know what was going through my head really when I put it in [the box], but it has two different ends and this [holds up the cable] connects them and ... [pause].
>
> **Jack** (aged 16): Perhaps it means that the different ends ... [pause]. Like everyone's a different person ... [pause].
>
> **Amy**: But like they are all connected by... [pause].
>
> **Jack**: By death.
>
> **Amy**: Yes, by death. Because everybody dies regardless of who you are. If you're rich or really poor or you're really fat or you're really thin, everybody dies ... [pause followed by silence].

The Positives and Negatives of Death

Having reviewed the inevitability of death alongside the fear and avoidance this sometimes raises for young-people, for their relationships with adults and for society more generally, the possibility of positive, as well as negative aspects of death, were also considered. From a positive perspective, this was not just the acceptance of death as discussed in the previous section but an analytical approach, which considered death within positive frameworks, as good, as transforming and as giving meaning to life. In contrast, death was positioned as particularly negative when young-people reflected upon the potential death of their parents, an aspect of mortality they seemed keen to interrogate. Henry (aged 17), like many of these young-people, combined both positive and negative approaches to death in his unique evaluation, structured within his own personal framework of everyday life experiences, associated with, what he calls, a series of 'small deaths'.

On a positive note, Charlotte (aged 15) questioned if death is always a bad thing, and discussed her response through the artistic interpretation of her box.

> **Charlotte**: Anyway another thing I wanted to say was that I've painted my box black on the outside and like better colours on the inside [bright blue].
>
> **Sally** (aged 15): [Looking inside the box] That's glitter.
>
> **Megan** (aged 15): Oh the glitter, that's so pretty.
>
> **Charlotte**: That's because on the outside I thought, and everyone always says death is like sad and gloomy, but then if you look into it and see that someone had an amazing life, then it's not so sad.

Charlotte points out that in conjunction with 'everyone' she had considered death to be 'sad and gloomy', however, on reflection, and in terms of someone who has had an 'amazing life', she asserts that death may be seen in a different light. Without clarifying the term 'amazing life', she suggests that it is possible to see death as 'not so sad'. Charlotte initially positioned herself within the negative discourse of death seeing it as bleak, blank and black but upon further consideration emerges with a different story. The story was not embellished upon, but the deep azure blue of the interior of the box and the sparkling glitter illuminated another, more optimistic, perspective on the age-old question of mortality.

Amy supports Charlotte's view, and also affirms that death can be good as it gives a purpose and meaning to life.

Amy: Oh I forgot about this [shows a picture of a thumbs up] because death is good, because it gives purpose to life, which fits in with the conversations we've just had. And earplugs [lifts earplugs out of the box] because I don't really like listening to sad stuff about death because it depresses me and makes me think about my death, which I'd rather not. I'd rather get on with my life than wallowing in death, so I brought some earplugs so that I don't have to listen about death all the time. I don't really watch the news because I'd rather have a happy life than a sad life.

However, following on from this initially positive affirmation, in which death gets a 'thumbs-up', Amy produces a pair of earplugs to suggest that she does not want to hear about it, as it makes her sad. By accommodating both an understanding of death as potentially good whilst at the same time not wanting to think about it continuously, Amy asserts that concentrating on life rather than death is a better approach. Amy continues to expand her ideas with the help of Laura (aged 15), and Jack (aged 16).

Amy: I've brought a picture of a bored person.

Laura: Why? Are you bored? [All laugh].

Amy: No it's because [shows picture], I think she has hair like me [laughs].... because if you never die there wouldn't be any new people and you would be very bored and obviously if you die and you're still hanging around somewhere you might be bored, cos I like doing stuff. So without death, life would be really boring because there would be no meaning if it goes on forever and ever.

Jack: There is no drive for you to do stuff if you have an endless amount of time.

Amy: If stuff runs out then you're going to use it more, it's going to be more valuable to you. You savour the stuff that's going to run out. I mean like if you have a whole bar of chocolate you just eat it, but if I have a little bit left then I like to eat it in small bits because I don't want it to run out. If you think that works as an analogy.

SC: I think that works well. Chocolate as a metaphor for life and death.

Amy: Also if you had an endless amount of chocolate you probably just wouldn't want it anymore.

Laura: I know someone who worked at Thornton's chocolate, actually making the chocolates and she didn't like chocolate after a while, but that's ok cos now she works at a shampoo factory. [All laugh].

Amy continues with the idea that death brings meaning to life, via her reflections on how boring life would be if everyone lived forever and potentially how dull death might be if there is nothing to do. That life and time are limited resources for humans, encourages Jack and Amy to consider the value of both, savouring each moment and experience, like the last piece of a bar of chocolate. This metaphor provides Amy, Jack and Laura with an opportunity to expand upon and appreciate the importance of life and death. They question; if life was an endless commodity would you still want it so much or is it because of its limited nature that we place such value on time and the human lifespan.

Similarly, Charlotte (aged 15) considers some of these points further and suggests that being aware of death makes her value time, existence and her approach to life more seriously.

Charlotte: I heard, I don't know if it was a TV show or something, that 'life only has meaning because it ends'. So it makes death like, well what's the point, what's the point of doing something well, what is the point of having fun, cos you know you could do it anytime. But … because of death you have to squeeze a huge amount of life out of what is a relatively short amount of time in some people's cases, and you know you've got so much to do, every day, every hour, every minute you've got something to do, and I kind of like to think that I live my life by trying to do everything I can. I was talking to my sister about this this morning and she said, I think she said the Celts, they used to act as though it was a funeral when someone was born cos like there are these two worlds and they are like interlinked in death and birth, and when somebody dies in this world they are born in the other world. Every time there was a birth there was a death in the other world and every time there was a death in this world there was a birth in the other world. So they didn't make it feel so bad.

Charlotte uses the story she has heard to link life and death together. Yet even with such a positive account a trace of uncertainty appears to linger. It seems that these young-people believe death can have positive elements that encourage people to value time and life, and that this limited existence gives meaning to the lives we lead. However, as William James (1902) states,

> Let sanguine healthy-mindedness do its best with its strange power of living in the moment and ignoring and forgetting, still the evil background is really there to be thought of, and the skull will grin in at the banquet' (in Becker 1973: 16)

What if Your Parents Die?

Davies argues that 'parenthood is challenged when a child dies' (2002: 12), and likewise it would appear that childhood is challenged when a parent dies. One of the most negative aspects of death that young-people from across the age groups reflected upon was the possibility of parental or close family loss. This was viewed, in the words of Megan (aged 15) as 'the most heart rending ever'. It seems that this is a particularly hard area for the young-people to consider, yet it dwells as a potentially prominent feature within their landscapes of death. Such an emotional and bleak feature calls for an exploration.

Tom (aged 10) opens-up these conversations, as he considers how he might respond to this unsettling situation.

> **Tom:** A few months ago I was thinking about death because I sometimes have these thoughts about … What if Mum and Dad die? And how I might react and stuff. I end up thinking that it's going to be quite a long time, because I feel like I've been alive for absolutely ages and I'm only 10, so I think I've got an awful long time to go, so I stop imagining when I'm going to grow up because then Mum and Dad would be getting older. [Silence]. Well, if they did die I'd feel really bad but then I'd try to think of the good things.

Tom clearly finds the death of his parents a difficult prospect to encounter and rehearses what he might do in the event of their death. He defends himself from these thoughts by considering a number of factors; first his age, 'I'm only ten', and therefore it should be a long time until his parents die, he even stops thinking about growing up himself as this scenario leads to his parents being older and potentially nearer to death. The silence within this short extract, speaks almost as loudly of Tom's concerns, as his words. It is clearly a difficult place for him to be, so much so that he has to turn towards more positive images in order to move on.

Justine (aged 10) also takes a brief look at the possibility of close family death.

Justine: [Holds up photographs of her family; one with all her family, one of her oldest sister and one with herself and her father. On a piece of paper, she has written: What if they die?]. I just wonder what will happen if they die. [Silence].

Charlie (aged 10): Yes, because if say your Mum dies, then you think who do you go with, do you go and live with you Dad or your Step-Dad.

Justine: Yes, because if my brother and me went to live with our Dad he might not have enough money to look after us because he only looks after himself and things like that. I wonder what would happen. [Further silence].

Again there is a silence as Justine considers this terrible possibility. She both writes and verbalises the question that she poses but cannot answer, 'what if they die'? At this point, it is not clear if she is referring to the family, herself, or both. Perhaps feeling under pressure to solve the issue for his friend, Charlie interjects with a practical solution, which only leads to further questioning from Justine. She considers the potential of this new situation but returns again to her question, 'what will happen'? The question hangs in the air, silence follows and nobody makes any further attempt to answer it.

It is clear that young-people do think about the issues presented above and consider a variety of different scenarios and questions. The questions are hard and the answers even harder to find, but if young-people ask them perhaps we, as adults, should listen, that is if young-people want us to. As previously considered, St Vincent Millais' poem opines the adult view that 'Childhood is the kingdom, where nobody dies', particularly focusing on, 'Nobody that matters that is'. Arguably this is not the case for young-people, not in reality and not in their own inner worlds. Their deathscapes include, if not a kingdom, a space where people that matter do die, questions are asked and a search for meaning begins. Research, for example Ribbens McCarthy (2006), has tended to and quite understandably so, focus on children who are bereaved and the impact this has on their lives. I contend that although a great many young-people may not have experienced the actuality of death and loss, it is a very present part of their everyday lives. Contained within their own internal deathscapes, these potential deaths and bereavements exist, and the emotions and feelings that may accompany them. Death exists quietly in these places, relatively undisturbed and unobserved. Perhaps by listening, we can begin to understand the depth and complexity of these spaces and begin to unravel the importance of what dwells there.

Similar conversations persist with a group of 15-year-old girls, who continue the exploration of parental death and pose some further questions. However, the focus shifts from how they, as young-people, might feel and cope with the death of their parents to how parents might cope with the death of a child. A variety of complex ideas are taken into consideration.

Megan: I always find the idea of having to bury my parents as the most heart-rending thing ever; because they can't die, they're my parents.

Charlotte: It's like when we were watching the Lion King.

Megan: Oh my God yes.

Sally: It's like when the King dies and Simba says 'you promised me you'd always be there and you lied', and that's like [hesitates]. How do they cope with that? I mean losing those you love, your parents. I think if your parents do die like when you are our age it must be really like awful because you've grown up with them and known them. If you lose your parents when you are a baby it never seems as bad because you had never known them and you never had that connection to them.

Charlotte: Yes, they never went through your entire life helping you and being with you … [Short silence].

All: [Begin to agree]. Yes. Yeah. [Nodding heads].

At this point, the girls seem to be in agreement that losing a parent would be the hardest thing that could ever happen. Then Ellie reconsiders, and attempts to view this through the eyes of a parent losing a child, are made.

> **Ellie:** I feel worse for parents who have lost their children, rather than children who have lost their parents.
>
> **All:** Why?
>
> **Ellie:** Well, even if adults can cope with it better, I heard someone say it was completely unnatural for adults to have to bury their child because parents aren't supposed to outlive their children. It's expected that when you have a child, the child will outlive you. It doesn't seem right that you bring something into the world and then have to send them out of the world.
>
> **Charlotte** My Mum said to me 'don't die before me because I couldn't live without you'.

Charlotte's final words offer a new perspective from those discussed thus far. However, it echoes the young-people's feelings and responses. The sentiments of Charlotte's mother, 'don't die before me because I can't live without you', are the mirror image of the young-people's views when looking at parental death. These highly emotional words, and the sharing of them, demonstrates the connections and interconnections of young-people's private deathscapes with those of others. The connectivity provides the opportunity for alternative viewpoints to be recognised and empathy and sympathy shared.

I leave the final words it this section to Lottie, Tom and Milly (aged 10), and Justine (aged 11). In this short conversation they contemplate the deaths of mothers and babies and wrestle with the complicated dilemma of which is worse, the mother or the baby dying. The sadness and complexity of this engages them as they thoughtfully reflect upon this difficult situation.

> **Lottie:** I worry though because sometimes if you have a baby the mother dies and the baby lives [hesitates], or the baby dies.

Tom: I think it's worse if the mother dies, it means the baby's got dad, but it's worse without the mother. [Silence].

Milly: Maybe it's better if the baby dies. [Thoughtful silence].

Justine: They could make another one. [Thoughtful silence].

Milly: If the mum dies you can't make another one. [Silence].

Reflections on Life as a Series of Small Deaths

Interestingly, one young man, Henry (aged 17), viewed particular experiences within his everyday life as, in his words, 'small deaths'. These small deaths give meaning to his life in much the same way as actual death is suggested to give meaning to human existence, and help him to understand his changing relationships and the transformative qualities of his everyday experiences in creating new beginnings for himself. Whilst the stories he tells relate directly to his life, they reposition death within the context of small everyday events rather than one cataclysmic occasion. Henry's small deaths share a striking resemblance with other young-people's views, in that death gives meaning to life, can transform and change lives both positively and negatively, and is sad but equally brings new hope and new possibilities. Reflecting in this way sets life and death on a more equal footing, rather than in opposition to each other. It highlights more specifically deaths inextricable link to the everyday lives of young-people. Both life and death therefore can share meaning and purpose or emptiness and boredom, neither one can be viewed as wholly good or wholly bad but both are undoubtedly complex, potentially transformative and part of our individual and collective stories.

Henry: I'd like to explain how I see life as a series of little deaths through some of the objects I have brought, and I've brought lots.

Henry's accounts are brief and often entertaining stories that caused great amusement amongst his peers. However, they adopt an increasingly serious and thoughtful tone as he moves from wider societal issues to personal friendships and finally to the 'death' of his first serious relationship. His accounts take on the quality of a life history as he guides us through his observations. Henry speaks about happiness, sadness, anger and moving forward, unconsciously mimicking traditional theories of grief, which include stages of anger, denial, bargaining and acceptance, similar to those proposed by Kubler Ross (1969/ 2009). Through his discussion of life's ordinary events, links to death are made in a very accessible and human way. Henry begins with the death of his belief in consumerism and capitalism.

Henry: First of all, I have this Starbucks mug that I stole from Leeds [laughter]. Sorry, I meant to say, 'bought' [emphasises word], in Leeds. This symbolises my death in the interest of consumerism [laughter continues]. Which is only true to a point, but I no longer shop at Starbucks or buy expensive clothes unless someone else is paying [laughter]. It's the death of my belief in the capitalist system and in consumerism.

He continues with the demise of his belief in the education system.

This is an extract from my school planner in year 11. It says… [Mimics teacher's voice] … 'I was disgusted at Henry's behaviour in church, talking, laughing and dancing during the year presentations. I expect far better from him and so does the school and I would have thought he would have had more respect for himself and his peers'. [Continues in his own voice but with a mocking tone] This is not only extremely scandalous for my good self but symbolises the death of my conformity to arrogant bastard teachers who insist you have five stripes on your tie. And in fact I wasn't dancing I was doing 'the cardboard box' to 'Hark the Herald Angels Sing' [laughter]. It's like death, it makes you really cross.

Henry indicates that these two 'small deaths' influence his feelings towards life and death. The anger he feels at attempts made by organisations to control his life, and the antagonism towards these small, petty, everyday constrains links closely to his anger of and around death itself, and arguably the power they and it have over him. Davies (2002) argues that death challenges not only the cessation of an individual's identity but also society, its structures, beliefs and attitudes. This combination of ideas is played out in Henry's reflections. His seemingly random ideas in relation to Starbucks and being 'told off' at school, bring together and challenge the societal structures in which he lives, his own personal stories and individuality, and his feelings in relation to life and death.

At this point Henry's focus shifts to the importance of personal relationships and how each of these has been a small death. He starts with the death of his childhood.

> My childhood died the day I signed up to MSN Messenger [all laugh]. I used to have this friend who I met on vampirefreaks.com [more laughter], and I arranged to meet him in Manchester and he stood me up [hesitates]. So that's when my childhood died [hesitates again]. I've had many more people stand me up since then but he was the first.

Despite the humorous elements of Henry's account, a sense of loss and reflection is pervasive. This perhaps ordinary and commonplace experience within the teenage years of being 'stood-up' by a potential boyfriend or girlfriend evokes, for Henry, the loss of his childhood and the carefree and innocent images that accompany it. The realisation of this loss is experienced with sadness and acceptance but the impact remains in a similar way to the death of a loved friend. Continuing, Henry discusses the death of his life as a straight teenager.

> This vanilla wooden ball belonged to [name] and he was my first partner in the gay world. So, I suppose this symbolises the death of my life as a straight young teenager.

His response to this death is more assertive, more accepting and more empowering, as he recognises that this event transformed his life.

Finally, in a moving account, Henry turns to the death of his first serious relationship.

> I'll read it first and then explain what it is cos it might be quite sensitive to a certain person in the group. [Looks questioningly at a specific member of the group who nods assent but says nothing. Henry takes a piece of paper from the box and reads] ... 'I can't do it anymore because it seems to me that there is no trust left. I think if you had just said the

truth when it happened I would be fine. I am going to protect my heart rather than be happy. I love you so much that my walls come down and if you did what you did when drunk I don't think I could cope with that again. Sorry, but I need security. [Pauses, looks up from letter and continues]. This letter symbolises the death of the only serious relationship I have ever had.

Mike (aged 17): It's like 'Sex and the City'. [Some uneasy laughter from the group]

Henry: At the turn of the year 2008/9, I cheated on the person who I was having a serious relationship with and from then on there was no trust and it steadily went downhill until the eventual end of it which was about six weeks ago. And this [holds paper in front of him] symbolises the death of a relationship but also the start of a new life for me, where I am looking. [Some laughter]. I've made a lot of friends since then, I'm not saying it was a particularly good death, or a particularly good new beginning, but the fact remains that I have changed and grown as a person … [Hesitates, silence].

Susie (aged 17): So you're saying that death is not just the end of something but can be a new beginning.

This account was particularly moving for Henry and one other specific member of the group, but equally for everyone present. Clearly detailed and graphic in its construction of the love and loss of a meaningful relationship, it also symbolises to Henry that both life and death can be a potentially new beginning. Life and death are not always good but they have the power to lead to change.

Within all these accounts, everyday stories of life are privileged over direct accounts of death. Death is made visible to Henry and us, in a way that perhaps staring into the abyss does not. Situating death amongst life and the living and the everyday events of our existence, emphasises more clearly the human reflections and responses to it, be they negative or positive. It some ways these reactions are more keenly felt when dealt within a context we understand, rather than questioning our mortality via complex existential theorising. Henry's small deaths reflect the presence of death within his and our everyday lives with great clarity. His accounts mirror both the affirming and the negative views of previous conversations and incorporate his personal search for meaning in the face of death, whilst looking at the bigger picture of his own life.

What Happens After Death?

Jo (aged 15) introduces this section by recounting the tale of 'the water nymph and the dragonfly' to her friends Ruth, Helen and Lucy (all aged 15). In so doing she illustrates her belief that what happens after death is unknowable.

> **Jo**: You know the story, the story where the water nymph turns into a dragonfly and can't go back to tell them what happens.
>
> **Ruth, Helen and Lucy**: No
>
> **Jo**: Well, the water nymph lives under the water at the bottom of the pond for most of its life. So when it grows up it starts to crawl up a stem and out of the water, and says to the other water nymphs I'll come back and tell you what happens. But, when it's dried out, and its new wings have formed and everything it can't go back under the water, so the rest of the water nymphs will never find out. That's like our death; nobody can come back and tell you what happens so we'll never know.

Jo is certain that humans cannot know what happens after their death but this did not stop the exploration of a range of possibilities. It was clear that some young-people held strong beliefs about an afterlife, often expressed and explained through religious frameworks. However, other notions were not always so clear-cut or expressed with such certainty, instead containing a variety of religious, spiritual and supernatural concepts alongside of scientific thoughts. The suppositions concerning an afterlife lead to colourful opportunities for the exploration of multiple possible spaces and encounters one might experience after this life has ended. A variety of reflections support Schleifer's view that,

> children readily accept both the supernatural and the biological conceptions of death. This is because children are not "materialists". Their

experiences have lead them to their own "theory" of mind that is incompatible with the idea that physical matter is the only or fundamental reality. (2011: 133)

An Afterlife?

Religious frameworks have been, and perhaps still are, central to perceptions of an afterlife. Nearly fifty years ago Berger (1967) positioned religion as a 'sacred canopy', a shelter under which humans strive to make sense of their mortality. Howarth (2007) agrees, suggesting that premodern societies made sense of death through religious doctrine and by situating an afterlife and therefore the continuation of life as a certainty. Despite the clear and incontestable evidence that an active human becomes a 'passive corps', human cultures have nevertheless 'universally asserted that something of the individual continues after death' (Davies 2002: 5). The following conversations highlight the continued use of religious perspectives and concepts in attempts to make sense of life's end, and the dominance of these in perceptions of an afterlife. Then again, the young-people also illustrate the changing and fluid nature of such notions.

Laura and Amy (both aged 15) and Jack (aged 16) begin by discussing their views of what happens after death. Laura has a clear impression of what heaven and hell mean to her. Her image of hell lacks the traditional implications of eternal damnation and punishment, and instead is simply a place without God. Jack, who describes himself as a Christian, tentatively agrees with Amy's picture of heaven and hell but with less certainty. Initially, he suggests a belief in an afterlife but proceeds to question this understanding, interpreting it as 'a guess', before returning to his previous opinions. Jack continually reflects upon and questions his ideas. In contrast, Amy makes it clear from the start that she has 'not got a clue' about the afterlife. She concludes, that she is not afraid to die but wants to make the most of her life 'just in case there's nothing else'.

Laura: I also brought a cross and a Bible to show you my ideas about death and that you go to heaven or hell after you die. I don't think that heaven and hell are like two separate places, it's just that heaven is somewhere like where God is and hell somewhere where he's not. If you say people are like going to hell it's not necessarily like a punishment or anything, it's just they have lived their whole life without God so why would they want to live their afterlife with God, so they go somewhere without God. It's not necessarily bad.

Jack: I think I believe in that too because I'm a Christian but I don't think it makes anything about death easier because you don't know what it is. Although I believe in it it's still just a guess and you don't have any clue what it's going to be like. You see the only thing you're used to is things that 'are', like your friends and family, and once you die you don't know what happens, even though I do believe like you go to heaven or hell.

Amy: Well, I don't have a clue. I'm not afraid of dying it's just that if there is nothing afterwards I would like to make the most of my time when I'm alive.

Despite taking different positions, Laura, Jack and Amy share their views confidently. Laura's interpretation of an afterlife is definite, Jack is less assured in his affirmation of heaven and hell, and likewise Amy exhibits a lack of certainty. However, whilst re-affirming her non-religious position, Amy brings a Bible out of her box and reflects upon how influences within her environment have potentially led her to 'adopt' some religious ideas into her understanding.

Amy: I've brought a Bible as well. I'm not very religious but I always seem to associate death with heaven or hell or religion in general. I think it's because I've grown up with it. My Mum's a Christian and at primary school we were always praying in assembly and stuff, so that Christianity was around me all of the time and I sort of adopted it a bit and... [hesitates]. I don't really know ... I think it's just been around me. At funerals they always talk about God and stuff.

Jack: Is it because you think that when people talk about death they think about what is going to happen after death and that's normally to do with religion? If you're going to go anywhere after death, it's normally to do with religion where you're going. Quite a lot of things that worry you are not to do with religion until you die and then you go to heaven with

God. But quite a lot of people don't think about religion until they die and then you think about going to heaven.

Jack responds to Amy by linking death with religious thoughts and therefore the subsequent aspirations of an afterlife. He speculates that religion only becomes an issue for many people when they think about death and what might happen after it. Although many of these conversations reveal some firmly held beliefs in an afterlife and an equal amount of uncertainty, the links between death and life-after-death have a tendency to be situated within religious and/or spiritual contexts. Whilst Beit-Hallahmi (2011: 52) asks 'could any ideology other than religion enable humans to face death' (2011:52), these conversations reveal that although young-people might think it is important, they simultaneously explore the challenges it raises. Amy, who has questioned and wrestled with a number of ideas during this conversation, now seems to welcome her ambiguity, as she ponders the difference between her brother's surety and her uncertainty.

Amy: My brother thinks that when you die, that's it, and there's nothing else happens. I think that's quite bad that he's so sure and that he's not open to the possibility that a part of you might live on in a different way.

Amy considered, challenged and re-evaluated her position throughout these converstions. Confronted by her brother's assured post-death non-existence she questions his conviction of nothingness with her possibilities and potential for a different life. Although Amy's deliberations, alongside those of her friends, suggest the continued presence of traditionally Christian concepts in relation to their beliefs and constructions of an afterlife, they also establish changing, shifting and questioning approaches. The following section explores these further, uncovering hybrid combinations of both traditional religious views with scientific perspectives that suggest no such thing as an afterlife.

No Afterlife?

Reflections on concepts such as blackness, nothingness, mystery and the unknown were, in the words of these young-people, 'scary'. However, this did not stop the exploration of them. Many of the discussions were not comforting or supportive of immortality, yet they indicated an engagement with contemporary debates within and between religion and science, which continue apace. Thus, the conversations frequently alternate and move back and forth between arguments related to something and/or nothing. First, a group of predominantly 15-year-old boys, discuss the possibility that there is 'nothing' after death and link this to scientific theories of the beginning of the universe.

> **John**: Well I printed these off this morning. [Takes pictures out of his box]. One's a picture of a black hole, and I thought like, a black hole's like a big mystery and no one knows exactly what it is so it's like a big unknown.
>
> **Syed**: And that's the same with death.
>
> **John**: Yeah so no one knows what's after it and … [hesitates].
>
> **Syed**: And it sounds scary
>
> **Ted**: Yeah, like in physics today we were talking about the beginning of time and like the Big Bang and I think that's really scary.
>
> **John**: Yeah, just black, just nothing.
>
> **Ted**: I think it's like if there is nothing after you die you'd miss out on everything good that's going to happen, like deep space travel and landing on Mars and stuff. But the thought of being immortal is not good either because it might be boring.

Finding these reflections somewhat problematic the boys extend their ideas.

> **John:** It doesn't seem real that like you go through life and then that's it; everything's done. In my opinion I can't see that happening. Just like everything else recycles, I reckon as soon as you die you're like maybe born again. I can't think you just die out; it's more like a process you go through.
>
> **Syed** Yes, they say you have like a year after dying and then you get reincarnated as something better.

Chris (aged 14): I'm not like a really big believer in God and stuff but I like to think there's a heaven and a hell.

John: Yeah, I'm with you on that.

Nothingness was clearly regarded as a possibility but not one the boys wanted to dwell on exclusively. Both afterlives that included 'nothing' and also potentially 'something' were incorporated into their reflections as possible experiences. Even those who professed not to be believers in God or an afterlife liked to think, or perhaps hope, that there might be one in some form or another, allowing the concepts of nothing and something to exist side by side. The existence of such views are hardly surprising in an era where young-people have access to both knowledge of complicated quantum physics and of religious traditions. A world in which, as Schleifer (2011) points out, contemporary scientific facts and theories are just as difficult to get to grips with as explanations of God, and that there is little to distinguish between 'God' talk and 'infinite multiverse' talk with regard to its complexity. Notwithstanding such difficulties these four boys skilfully consider and integrate talk of God and a presumed afterlife, with scientific ideas that predominantly position an afterlife as an impossibility.

Similarly, a group of 15-year-old girls go on to explore the fear of nothingness and why believing in something is, in the words of Lucy, 'a comfort'.

Lucy: I think it's easier for people to believe in a heaven or a hell because like in RE [Religious Education] we learnt about the reasons why people should believe in an afterlife, that is, it's easier for people to cope with death if they believe people have gone somewhere afterwards. Whereas for me I'd rather go to hell than go nowhere, because the idea of there being nothing, absolutely nothing terrifies me. But the idea of going to hell doesn't as much because at least there's something. And sometimes I think it's a comfort for people to think there's something there, rather than not know. It lets you come to terms with death. It's just the idea of it stopping. I can't imagine it all just stopping indefinitely. Not being able to have thought, I .... [Hesitates].

Helen: If there's nothing though, it doesn't matter.

Lucy: Yeah I know, but it's just this idea of nothing [Pause]. Cos like at night when it's dark and there's no sound I can sort of imagine and think what it might be like [short silence]. I'm frightened to die having done nothing with my life or dying young scares me cos I won't have been able to grow up and do all sorts of things.

Jo: My brother says, 'live fast, die young and leave a beautiful corpse'. I think that's silly, I think living fast and dying old is a much better idea.

Lucy's dread of 'nothing' is palpable, no life, no thoughts, everything stopping forever, nothing. She suggests that at night, in the dark, she can begin to imagine what nothingness might be like. Her thoughts of being young and having done nothing with her life combine with the terror of finding nothing after it, and then she is afraid to die. In this poignant moment the reassurance of life after death falls away and finitude is starkly realised. It is at this point that Jo steps in to support her friend, implying that dying young is unlikely and that 'living fast and dying old' are, in her view, the better option. She suggests therefore that 'death cannot be abolished but it can be delayed' (Beit-Hallahmi 2011: 44). Extending this argument further, Beit-Hallahmi asserts that biomedical technology 'has eliminated the connection between death and childhood' (2011: 56) by extending life and distancing young-people from death. From a contemporary Western stance, surely he is correct, the physical connectedness between children, young-people and death has been stretched. However, Lucy's words suggest a psychological connection and presence, which remains and goes on.

Possibilities?

The following section features 'possibilities'. The likelihood of an afterlife and, if it exists, what opportunities it might provide. The following conversations feature a rich variety of colourful and sometimes amusing scenarios, beliefs and imaginings. Personal and intimate inner landscapes of death are generously shared, and through their stories we encounter death and search for meaning and understanding alongside of these young-people. We begin with a group of predominantly ten-year-old children who observe what life-after-death might be like. Their ideas move swiftly past traditional views of heaven and hell, through reincarnation, to the possibility of life returning after death.

Justine (aged 11): I have something I wonder about with death, it's whether you go to heaven or hell.

Lottie: I think that when you die you might become a different person or an animal or something.

Charlie: When I die I might come back as a cherry. I don't think I'd want to be a cherry. It must be quite a boring life just stuck to a tree until someone comes-by and picks you … and eats you… [All laugh]

Milly: How do you know? Are you a cherry? I heard they were going to make baby mammoths out of something. They take something from a mouse and inject it with something they found from a baby mammoth frozen in the ice, and they were going to turn it into an alive one.

Tom: They made a programme on it, called *Waking the Baby Mammoth*. They showed like what happened to the baby mammoth before it died, and they could maybe inject it and bring it back to life. It's like everything had been preserved together, so maybe they could make another one.

Justine: Yes, I heard they've got this thing where you can freeze your body and bring it back to life in the future. So you wouldn't really die. It's like the mammoth.

Diverse post-life options and possibilities are presented and considered. All are colourful and expansive. Charlie suggests that, once dead, he may return to life as a cherry, although he thinks this might be a potentially boring afterlife. More exciting to these younger children is the possibility of bringing mammoths back to life, after they have been frozen in the ice for centuries. Here Milly suggests that they could make 'an alive one'. Even more alluring is Justine's supposition that it is not only mammoths that can be returned to life but humans also, thereby not dying at all. Justine's views alter dramatically throughout the conversation; beginning with a traditional choice of heaven or hell and ending with the possibility of not dying at all. These kaleidoscopic ideas are alluring, they reveal serendipitous and yet jointly created thoughts and ideas, establishing richly ornate, plentiful and transforming landscapes of death.

Tom (aged 10) gives an equally curious and amusing view of the afterlife.

> **Tom:** It might be a bit weird, but [hesitates]. Well I think about death like, when you die you die, but sort of like you wake up almost, but when you wake up you wake up above the clouds. Then there's like this gigantic desk, and you go through the gate and then there are three chairs, one with God in, one with Jesus in and one empty, and then you see like heaven and it's just like this but much better.
>
> **SC:** Whose is the empty chair?
>
> **Tom:** I don't know, I just thought that Jesus sits on the right hand side of God.
>
> **Millie:** It could be for the Holy Spirit.
>
> **Tom:** He wouldn't need a chair he'd just be twirling around the lights. [All laugh]

Tom's account and creative solution to why the Holy Spirit would not need a chair amused everyone. Tom is clearly well versed in time-honoured, Christian concepts and images of Heaven. He deftly incorporates these into his construction. However, he does not passively accept these but smartly assembles them into his own original and more diverting view of immortality.

A group of older teenagers demonstrate further creativity and amusement when Amy and her friends explore the possibility of meeting famous people in the afterlife.

> **Amy** (aged 15): I've got a picture of Ben Shepherd because if I do [die], and I end up in some other place, then I'd like him to be there because I adore him in every way.
>
> **SC:** Who is Ben Shepherd?
>
> **Amy:** He's a television presenter.
>
> **SC:** Does everyone know who Ben Shepherd is?
>
> **Jack (aged 16):** Oh blooming hell!! Don't I know who he is!! [Both girls laugh loudly]

Amy: Yeah well, I like him and I'd like to meet him sometime.

Laura: [Laughs]

Amy: Well we all know who she [Laura] wants to meet. Peter Petrelli that's Milo Ventimiglia. [Both laugh]

Jack: Looks skyward and shakes head]

Amy and Laura: [More laughing]

SC: So do you think it's possible that when you die you might meet these guys

Amy: No, I don't think so, but I'd like to. Maybe I'll meet them before I die.

On a more serious note, Jack explains why he think people like to believe they will be reunited with people after they die.

Jack: People have hope that maybe… heaven gives them the hope that they might be reunited with somebody rather than it just ending.

Laura: I don't know that when I die anyone will actually be there.

Jack: No, but it would good if they were. I'd like to meet the Beatles.

After Jack's assertion that it would be good to meet those you had known and loved in this life in the next one, the debate resumes. Whilst the argument continues to incorporate meeting others, the focus shifts to what might happen if you encounter those you do not wish to meet. This leads to philosophical theorising about the nature of paradise.

Laura: Oh I love them [The Beatles], but there might be people that you didn't want to see again and that you were glad had died.

Amy: But then it wouldn't be your heaven would it?

Laura: [Thoughtfully] No.

Amy: If your heaven is your kind of paradise then they wouldn't be there.

Laura: No, but then if your heaven is only your paradise then everyone would have a bit of heaven and then no one would ever meet.

Jack: Everyone's in the same heaven.

Amy: But then it's not my heaven if I have to walk around with someone I really loathe. Because then it's not my heaven it's more like hell, and I wouldn't like that.

Jack: No but you wouldn't necessarily meet them but they'd still be there, like I mean they might be on the other side of heaven.

Interestingly, whereas the younger groups' idea of heaven consists of colourful 'things', such as cherry trees and mammoths, the older teenagers' heaven is populated by people. Those they like and those they do not. It is these people that make heaven either a good place or a bad one. Amy suggests that heaven would be more like hell if people she dislikes in this life turn-up. Amy is clearly unsettled by these thoughts and continues to contemplate them. She considers what might happen if she had murdered someone and then met that person in heaven. Jack points out that in this case she would not be allowed into heaven because she was a murderer. However, taking the stance of repentance, Laura interrogates Jack's view and is amused at his inability to answer her.

Amy: If you are like someone who killed a person because you really hated them and then they were there when you got to heaven, wouldn't you be really like annoyed, cos you'd be like, well I killed you to get rid of you and now you'll be bugging me for all eternity.

Jack: Well if you killed somebody you wouldn't be in heaven.

Laura: What if you'd asked for forgiveness, like repented.
Jack: Well… [Laughs] … [Unable to answer Laura's questions]

[They all laugh].

This engaging array of changing and co-constructed debates, thoughts and ideas gradually draws to a close with Laura, Jack and Amy making their final points.

Laura: No wait, I know, I know, like in heaven there is no hate because that's bad.

Amy: Well that sucks, if everything you believed in on earth has suddenly disappeared when you go to heaven, I'd be really annoyed at that as well, then I'd be annoyed at heaven and that wouldn't be heaven.

Jack: Everyone who deserves to be there will be there and that makes it heaven.

Laura concludes that heaven is a place with no hatred and Jack that everyone who deserves to be there will be. Amy however, continues to be annoyed by the idea of heaven as a perfect place where everything will be different from her lived experience. This, she concludes, would not be heaven. Nevertheless, after some further thought, Amy again tries to make sense of one further possibility.

Amy: I read a book about *Alice in Wonderland*, it wasn't the original it was a weird one. She could control stuff with her imagination and she went to the *real world* by accident. She was about to marry this person and then got sucked back into her world. So she sent an imagined version of herself to be with her husband. So maybe in heaven you have the people there but they're not actually there. I don't know. So they are there but they are also in their actual heaven. It's difficult, it's like there's a copy of them.

Like *Alice*, Amy has been on a journey into strange and wonderful places, in which the complex, the everyday, the bizarre, the material, the existential, all meet together in one ordinary conversation of extraordinary ideas. Much like falling through the rabbit hole. These long discussions represent Amy's continually changing and complex views of a possible afterlife; 'heaven', 'paradise', 'eternity'. She asks complicated questions and equally complex answers are returned. Her view of heaven is connected to and populated by people, those people she wants to meet in an afterlife and those she 'loathes' and has no wish to meet ever again. Her paradise is rooted in those friends, beliefs and ideals, which she holds dear in this life and is annoyed by suggestions of different possibilities. Finally, Amy sees heaven and the people in it as 'copies' of their earthly selves. A deathscape in which she can re-establish her individual identity by surrounding herself by those people she loves and likes and distance herself from those she does not. In this way,

Amy copies and pastes herself into another world without losing herself in an idealistic view of heaven, which 'sucks'. Amy's final thoughts take her to yet more puzzling and perplexing spaces this time accompanied by copies, duplicates, simulacra. Like many of us faced with mutable, existential uncertainties, Amy acknowledges 'difficulties'.

Taking an equally philosophical approach to mortality, Isaac [aged 15] expressed his idea that 'we are all made up of dead people'. He explains that life and death consist of a continuous recycling of the atoms, the composition of which go into making human beings.

> **Isaac:** In here I have [rummages in the box] …I hope you don't mind me being 'sciency'. These are some of the weirdest things that you'll probably find in a box …these [he holds up a pairs of tweezers]. These, represent a tiny pair of tweezers, these are actually quite big tweezers. It's in a Bill Bryson book *A Short History of Nearly Everything*, and the introduction to this brings up the concept that if one was to pick oneself apart, although you'd probably have to get someone to help with the last stages, with a pair of nano-tweezers, atom by atom you'd end up with a pile of fine atomic dust that is you, has always been you, that has never been alive, but has supported life and is no longer alive, which I find is …
>
> **James:** Is a lot of information in a very small space of time…
>
> **Isaac:** Yes, but which I find is a very interesting concept, I think. The atoms that make up living things aren't alive, yet they support life in an integral, really complex structure, but then disperse once the organism has lived and then become other living things. It's a little bit weird to think that probably a large amount of your atoms have been somebody else's [all laugh] … But that's a little bit of a morbid thing to think about I suppose… [all laugh] … We're all made of dead people [all laugh] … Well all the atoms in me and in the earth are. Well, some are introduced and some are put out into space as junk, but all are recycled in essence in one continuous cycle of life and death, and I just find that entirely interesting as a concept, separate to the morbid and grievous side of death.

Isaac is a young man who is particularly interested in mathematics and science and his love of these topics has an impact on the way he thinks about life and death. His perspective, although essentially orientated around his passion for science, does not exclude the 'grievous' aspects of death but incorporates scientific knowledge with a cosmic and encompassing account of the continuous cycle of life and death.

It is clear that these young-people have explored the possibilities of an afterlife in great and creative detail. Images of heaven and hell were constructed and re-constructed, negotiated and argued. Individual and collective deathscapes were populated by colourful images and possibilities. The prospect of an afterlife was viewed through the appropriately different lenses of science, religion and philosophy. Some had already found satisfactory answers and meanings to the possibility of life after death and others had not. These highly expressive and creative reflections on beliefs, understandings and constructions of an afterlife were fascinating and alluring, and simultaneously created anew the questions, possibilities and answers that humanity shares when investigating, does anything happen after we die.

Conclusion

This chapter has presented ideas from across a broad range of existential issues. First, whilst death was positioned as inevitable, usual and unavoidable, nonetheless elements of fear, pertaining to both the young-people themselves and society as a whole, were recognised. The reaction to this fear was identified as a tendency to lie to oneself about the potential loss of loved ones, or to try and hide from death, the futility of which was equally familiar. Similarly, it was suggested that fear was communicated by adults, who in the eyes of these young-people, mistakenly attempt to protect them from facing or confronting the reality of death, which they see as unnecessary.

Second, death was constructed within both negative and positive frameworks, challenging commonly held assumptions that death is always bad. It was suggested that being vividly aware of one's own mortality and recognising that existence is time limited, means we value life more, and consequently death gives meaning to life. Death was viewed from a particularly negative standpoint when the death of parents was considered. Such deathscapes captured vivid pictures of parental loss and were often bleak places to venture into. However, these hidden spaces were very real and bravely shared, exposed, explored and reflected upon. Henry, combined both positive and negative aspects of life and death within his concept of 'small deaths'. His inimitable style and character, skilfully interweaved his life with elements of death, illustrating an unusual but readily recognisable and tangible version of death, which elevated it out of the coffin and into everyday experience.

Third, thoughts and ideas in relation to an afterlife were shared, considered and re-considered, forming ever changing and eclectic viewpoints. With no concrete evidence available to support or deny the existence of an afterlife, flexible approaches were adopted and individualised thinking combined with group ideas to create a myriad variety of thoughts. Traditional and non-traditional ideas of heaven and hell, plus the possibilities and practicalities of such a place or places, were discussed, and a preference for the inclusion of some form of continuation after life was popular, though not to be guaranteed. A major contributor to this, I suggest, was arguably not a fear and denial of death in the traditional religious sense, that is informed by body and soul and good and evil, but part of what the young-people identified as 'scary nothingness', a void in which there is no thought, no identity, nobody else, a total loss of self. Within this framework both concepts of 'nothing' and 'something', could and did exist side-by-side, incorporating the co-existence of both scientific and religious thinking in conceptualising, what might happen after death.

These young-people reflected upon existential debates and questions that have taxed humanity for centuries. The conversations revealed the broad arenas of death that their thoughts and ideas inhabit, discovered their inner deathscapes, and uncovered their ability to reflect upon and question their own ideas and those of others. In sharing, developing and co-constructing an array of differing philosophies, notions and ways of thinking with their friends, dynamic and changing responses to death were exposed.

Listening to these young-people brought their intricate compositions of death to light, as fact, as part of life, as a connection between all people, as a celebration of life and as potential for what may, or may not, come next. Adult assumptions that children should be protected from the reality of death, I suggest are misplaced, and prevent adults from listening to children about what matters to them. If, as adults, we listen to young-people's beliefs about death, perhaps we might hear that death is, as suggested by Professor Dumbledore in J.K. Rowling's *Harry Potter and the Philosophers' Stone* (1997), 'but the next great adventure'. Questions remain though, are we as adults ready to encounter the diverse and colourful deathscapes that young-people inhabit? Are we ready to wander together through these uncharted spaces and hear their reflections on their everyday encounters with death? Or will we remain silent, unapproachable and disinterested?

References

Becker, E. (1973). *The denial of death*. New York: The Free Press.

Beit-Hallahmi, B. (2011). Ambivalent teaching and painful learning: mastering the facts of life (?). In V. Talwar, P. Harris, & M. Schleifer (Eds.), *Children's understanding of death: From biological to religious conceptions*. New York: Cambridge University Press.

Berger, P. (1967). *The sacred canopy: Elements of a sociological theory of religeon*. New York: Doubleday.

Berridge, K. (2002). *Vigor mortis*. London: Profile Books.

Davies, D. J. (2002). *Death, Ritual and belief: Rhetoric of Funerary rites* (2nd ed.). London: Continuum.

Howarth, G. (2007). *Death and dying: A sociological introduction*. Cambridge: Polity Press.

Howells, C. (2011). *Mortal subjects: Passions of the soul in late twentieth-century French thought*. Cambridge: Polity Press.

Kubler Ross, E. (1969/ 2009). *On death and dying: what the dying have to teach doctors, nurses, clergy and their own families*. Abingdon: Routledge.

Maddrell, A., & Sidaway, J. D. (2010). *Deathscapes: Spaces for death*. Dying, Mourning and Remembrance, Surrey: Ashgate.

Ribbens McCarthy, J. (2006). *Young-people's experiences of loss and Bereavement: Towards an interdisciplinary approach*. Berkshire: Open University Press.

Schleifer, M. (2011). Thoughts and feelings: Children and William James have it right ! In V. Talwar, P. Harris, & M. Schleifer (Eds.), *Children's understanding of death: From biological to religious conceptions*. New York: Cambridge University Press.

Seale, C. (1998). *Constructing death: The sociology of dying and bereavement.* Cambridge: Cambridge University Press.

Wall, J. (2010). *Ethics: In the light of childhood.* Washington, DC: Georgetown University Press.

6

'We're OK with Death'

Introduction

I began this study with one specific aim in mind and that was to listen to young-people talk about death as part of their everyday lives. Perhaps an unlikely topic, which caused interest and suspicion in equal measure, from family, friends, colleagues and indeed the young-people themselves. Kastenbaum and Fox's (2007) assertion that adults assume, children cannot, do not and should not think about death was uppermost in my thoughts, and inspired me to enquire if indeed young-people can, do and perhaps more problematically should talk about death. My repeated consideration of this declaration, convinced me that at the very least young-people should be given the opportunity to have their say.

At the outset I worried if I was doing the right thing in carrying out research in this field. I reflected that adult assumptions might indeed be correct, and therefore my enthusiasm to promote the voices of young-people to the forefront of a potentially sensitive and emotive subject was, in fact, an intrusion into their lives, and a self-indulgence on my part. To a certain extent my anxiety was waylaid by my interest in these

© The Author(s) 2017
S. Coombs, *Young People's Perspectives on End-of-Life*,
Studies in Childhood and Youth, DOI 10.1007/978-3-319-53631-6_6

young-people, and a strong conviction that they would have plenty to say on the topic, if only given the opportunity. My confidence was rewarded through their forthright, unique and individual accounts of the presence of death in their everyday lives. I therefore use this concluding chapter to consider four key aspects, which go to make up these inspirational narratives. First, that death is a pervasive part of the everyday lives of these young-people. Second, that they extensively can and did think and talk about death. Third, that adult/societal anxieties, which construct death as profane when situated alongside the sacred nature of childhood, potentially position 'death and youth' as the last taboo. And fourth, in marked contrast to the previous assertion, that young-people are active creators of their own inimitable views on death.

Death in Everyday Life

In the concluding stages of her recent book, *Death in a Global Age*, McManus (2013) argues that death has the potential to be less certain in the near future, as advances in scientific research lead to the possible prolonging of life indefinitely and the subsequent questions that humanity will be faced with. For the present however, death in contemporary Western society remains a ubiquitous part of everyday life, both in highly public ways and more personal and private experiences. Death therefore is a part of young-people's lives and it would be naïve to think otherwise.

The conversations presented in this book have highlighted the omnipresent and highly visible nature of death in the daily lives of these young-people in a number of different ways. Death enters into their lives through a vast array of media sources, through personal encounters with death and as part of their inner thoughts and reflections on the topic. As exemplified within these conversations the deaths may not always be those of close family and/or friends, whose deaths were perhaps better known to previous generations of children, although arguably they still can be. Different kinds of deaths are now particularly visible, such as those outlined by Walter (2008) pertaining to the media, such as recent heroes and celebrities.

An initial analysis of the conversations reveals how, in particular, young-people are daily witnesses to a variety of high profile public images of death available through media sources, and equally frequent listeners and translators of cultural narratives that impact upon their knowledge and understanding of mortality. They seek out and communicate death related ideas via online forums, and are active mourners on Facebook, policing these virtual spaces and the tributes left there, with the same efficiency as any actual cemetery or council official.

Notwithstanding the ever-present influence of freely available media sources, more private and personal worlds have been uncovered, which contain frequent encounters with death through the seemingly routine loss of loved pets, and the impact of the not unusual death of relatives and friends. Whilst the title of St Vincent Millais' poem opines the familiar view that *Childhood is the Kingdom Where Nobody Dies*, the stories told portray death as a fairly regular occurrence in the everyday lives of these young-people. Although I did not set out to specifically uncover the issue of bereavement, different forms of loss were in fact fairly commonplace and elicited a variety of stories and a range of emotional responses.

The thoughtful and reflective notions encountered in the final data chapter revealed on-going inner contemplations of death. Appropriating Madrell and Sidaway's terminology, I referred to these as 'deathscapes' (2010), as they provided a view of dynamic, changing and colourful ideas. As questions of existence and non-existence were mooted, the amalgamation of personal thoughts and shared perspectives provided a view of some of the everyday anxieties and uncertainties that considering death brings with it. For example, what if my parents die? What if I die when I am still young? What if there is only 'nothingness' after death? And other similarly eclectic and stimulating responses.

The stories of impersonal public deaths and more personal private deaths are clearly prevalent and influential in the lives of these young-people and focus attention on the ordinary and everyday ways in which death makes itself apparent to them. Adult interpretations of death have tended to focus on the fear and anxiety death instils, rather than its ordinariness, and Silverman (2000), amongst others (Postman 1982, Elias 1985), contends that because of the propensity to cause such negative feelings, adults attempt to keep the potential disquiet of the subject away from children. I suggest that the contemporary and everyday nature of death discussed here struggles to do this, and that the conversations indicate that if this is the aim of adults and parents then they are failing. Death is an everyday occurrence, available to the young through their own poignant and personal experiences, their inner deathscapes of thoughts and reflections, and the ever-present media. Death is a part of everyday life and these young-people clearly recognise it.

Thinking and Talking About Death

Within the context of death as part of everyday life, it is clearly a wide-ranging topic that can be accessed and viewed through a number of different perspectives, such as literature, science, philosophy and religion. The ease and frequency with which these, and other, perspectives were utilised throughout the conversations, helped to undermine adult assumptions that young-people do not and cannot talk or think about the end-of-life. It became clear that the young-people did not only talk about death because they were specifically asked to do so as part of this study but also that they frequently engaged with the topic both directly and indirectly. For example, they pointed to death being indirectly referenced in relation to 'shoot-em-up' computer games, and conversely and more directly, when identifying and choosing songs to be played at their funerals.

A more detailed analysis, revealed not only the continued importance of public sources for everyday encounters with death but the private meanings and understandings they helped to develop. Amongst the many other spaces that death occupies in contemporary Western society, perhaps the media, personal memories and private musings, succinctly help to describe the arenas of death that these young-people felt comfortable to explore with each other, and equally the multiplicity of different viewpoints they exchanged. It is clear that these areas acted as a launch pad to enter into these discussions, and helped to uncover a wide ranging and far reaching ability to express their own individual stories.

The number and variety of media sources selected were significant in highlighting engagement with this topic. The inclusion of literature, film and other types of media representations were particularly prevalent, intriguing and exciting, and illustrated dominant cultural themes around death and dying, such as love, romance, heroism and violence. Drawn from both fantasy and reality and replete with references to prominent tropes within their own youth cultures; vampires and the undead, superheroes, celebrities, and knife crime, these accounts revealed a contemporary backdrop to death, via a rich and plentiful supply of cultural representations. The active development of these narratives provided a brief glimpse into the rich and colourful worlds of death that these young-people inhabit, and how through using such sources, more personal and unique stories emerged. Such a high level of engagement with the media, from across all the age groups, meant that frequent challenges to dominant cultural scripts were made. For example, the actual deaths experienced by the participants were discussed in sharp contrast to the romance, glamour and soft-focus of the cinema and the aesthetic and heroic depictions in teenage fiction, and instead were sources of anger, confusion and sadness. However, media sources were highly valuable in providing a salient context through which young-people could demonstrate agency in expressing their own views and experiences of death.

The highly public face of media deaths was arguably a safe place for young-people to begin their explorations of finitude, demonstrate awareness of it and uncover different ways of death. Indeed, throughout the conversations there was a tendency for all age groups to begin here. However, this pathway inevitably led to more personal and potentially emotional discussions, initially via challenges to the authenticity of media representations and then more directly through personal encounters with death detailed within evocative personal memories and stories.

One reason adults often give for not talking about death with children and young-people is the potential for this subject to be upsetting, and indeed I contend 'why would it be otherwise', especially in relation to deaths of personal friends or relatives. However, to avoid death altogether negates exploring a potential range of emotions and a rich diversity of contexts and stories, which would be missed if the opportunity to open up this topic was not given. A significant ability to communicate poignant stories was clearly expressed here, using a variety of emotions that incorporated the use of deeply felt silences, humorous performances and supportive gestures of both a physical and emotional nature. The positive verbal support offered by a group of fifteen-year-old boys to their friend, who had witnessed the dead body of his Grandfather, demonstrated this type of communication and understanding, and the moments when silence spoke for the emotions (we all felt), made powerful statements.

The majority of these young-people had encountered death, from much loved pets, to important and significant friends and relatives. Their memories of these people and the events surrounding their deaths were cherished and frequently expressed through material objects that came out of the shoeboxes. In this way precious memories were kept alive via the apparently ordinary and mundane but highly treasured and often evocative objects. To witness this 'stuff' being brought out of the boxes and the stories around them, from the blue ceramic dolphin belonging to Uncle Charlie, to the black shirt worn at a funeral, to 'words for Nan', alongside the generous offer to view Grandad's ashes, allowed death to be contemplated and shared, ideas to be exchanged and developed, friends to be supported, meanings constructed and the continued presence of the dead in their lives to be witnessed and valued.

Communicating arguments that relate to our existence and non-existence have never been easy. Chapter 5 shows young-people wrestling with such ideas and communicating their own personal views on the nature of mortality to their friends. This is not the safe ground shared through media stories, or the painful ground of personal stories where support from peers is readily available, this is contested and uncertain ground where ideas are often contentious. Religious beliefs and scientific knowledge can cause conflicting views that may situate the young person in opposition to their friends. However, individual attitudes, thoughts and understandings were communicated and ideas were often changed, considered and co-constructed within the conversations themselves. This was interesting to note, as was the complex and metaphorical way in which death was explained using abstract objects such as a

USB cable and a pair of tweezers. The complexity and multifaceted ways in which these young-people talked about death provides a creative and unique view of their own grand and expansive ideas and contributes new and previously unheard narratives to humanity's age old contemplation of death.

The detailed communication of these deathscapes was a testament to the participants' communication skills and their ability to think about death in terms of unique thoughts, co-constructed ideas, societal and individual influences and personal and shared experiences. It is clear to me that these young-people can and did talk about death but not only that, they did so eloquently, intuitively and creatively, producing rich, colourful and meaningful human stories that communicated their understanding and interpretation of death within their own terms of reference, thereby challenging the adult assumptions proposed by Kastenbaum and Fox. The question remains then: Just because they can and do talk about death, should they, or is this potentially the last taboo?

Death and Youth—the Last Taboo?

Although these conversations give a clear indication of the ability of these young-people to talk about death and the consummate way in which they do it, some studies attest to the fact that adults find talking to young-people about it difficult, since they arguably want to protect them from what they feel is a harsh and upsetting reality (Silverman 2000, Ribbens McCarthy 2006, Fearnley 2012). The presence of multiple and diverse narratives of death, both acknowledged and discussed in this book, suggest that adults may be fighting a losing battle and that as far as the young are concerned, death is already 'out of the box'. Although claims have been, and continue to be made, in relation to the universal fear of death, which is purported to lead to denial, sequestration and the taboo nature of the topic, others have argued that this is no longer the case and that death is a highly visible part of contemporary Western society, thus rendering the construction of a taboo as obsolete. However, if as Douglas contends, that societal systems of meaning are divided into, as her book title illustrates, *Purity and Danger* (1966/2002), cleanliness and uncleanliness, or the sacred and the profane, and the aim of society is to keep such opposing elements apart, we might contend that youth and death are indeed the final taboo.

In order to outline this suggestion more clearly I appropriate McManus's argument, which states that 'once something is imbued with a sacred status it is very important *never* to treat it as if it is profane as the profane defiles the sacred' (2013: 10). It has been argued within the covers of this text, both by myself and others, that the innocence of youth is a constructed and highly prized, indeed sacred, element in contemporary Western societies. In comparison, death is situated at the end of a long and fulfilling life, so need not touch the lives of the young. Faulkner's exploration of *The Importance of Being Innocent* (2011), argues that the young are protected from and denied knowledge of such things as politics, violence and sexuality, and here I include death. Childhood is therefore imbued with dominant societal attitudes, values and beliefs that contemporaneously identify the young as predominantly sacred objects, 'conceived in the model of divinity, as our sacred absolution' (Faulkner 2011: 24). Conversely, death is situated in opposition to this, as a threat, as a risk, as a dangerous profanity to this sacred potential. To reject this construction is to be seen to dismiss the child from childhood altogether. Douglas argues, that societal views of death and the corpse position them as dangerous because of their powers to contaminate the sacred, and because of their situation on the 'margins' (1966/2002: 150). She contends that 'all margins are dangerous' and similarly, 'if they are pulled this way or that the shape of fundamental experience is altered. Any structure of ideas is vulnerable at the margins' (1966/2002: 140). Aspects of both childhood and death are situated on these boundaries, often pulled to-and-fro, in-and-out of the limelight, as and when society dictates. I therefore suggest, that it is not at all surprising that societal/adult perspectives have trouble combining the two and that conversations between the generations are positioned as problematic. Youth and death are deemed unlikely companions, to be kept apart, for fear of contamination and the risk of upsetting young-people with realities they cannot yet cope with.

In response to such suggestions I contend that Faulkner's evaluation of Nietzsche's approach to innocence is important. Within this argument a different view of innocence is considered, which in opposition to the passive victim, gives rise to agency, choice and decision-making. Faulkner contends that 'if we subscribe too readily to the notion of innocent-to-be-protected, thus recoiling from suffering, then we also deny the possibility of freedom opened by the affirmation of becoming' (2008: 81–82). I contend therefore that we should not deny young-people the opportunity to talk about the end-of-life, as this study has clearly situated young-people as creative constructors of their own everyday worlds of death. In reconceptualising the construction of innocence in the light of agency, choice, creativity and empowerment, adults could more readily share in these conversations without fearing the restrictive taboo of 'not in front of the children'. Young-people themselves suggest that they should indeed talk about death and on this topic I leave the last word to Jack [aged 16],

> I think you should talk about it [death] because…[hesitates]… Just because you're young doesn't mean that it's not going to affect you, because there will be people around you that die at some point, and even if you're not … [hesitates]… or it's not your time to die that doesn't mean you shouldn't talk about it because of everyone else around you. [Hesitates] And people close to you will come and go.

Creative Constructors of Death

In conversation with young-people their stories, experiences, emotions and ideas relating to life and death were shared together through the use of everyday household objects. The stuff of everyday life was used as the starting point for this topic. The presence of ordinary, mundane objects, such as a kitchen knife, symbolised the loss of predominantly young life through knife crime, and hinted at anxieties surrounding death. Collections of more unusual objects were used to help elaborate and question intangible and abstract ideas. For example, a young man who was always losing his house keys and getting into trouble from his Mother for doing so, used them to explore feelings associated with loss and bereavement. Alternatively, a stopwatch was used to examine concepts of time, the finite nature of life and equally to question the possibility of infinite life. Objects that inspired memories and demonstrated on-going relationships with those who had died were plentiful. For example, Grandma's bell, an object specifically chosen from her Grandmother's house after her death, or a photograph of Granddad taken the Christmas before he died, or the swimming medals of a Great Grandfather who was never actually known in person but remains part of family history. A transcript of failed exam results, leading to the assertion 'I'm dead'. A love letter ending a first gay relationship. Bibles, novels, films, candles, tissues, words cut from newspapers, computer games, song lyrics, a truly amazing array of wonderful things.

Such everyday artefacts provided the basis for these remarkable discussions, a way of literally and metaphorically lifting the lid on death and taking a glimpse inside its confines. The methodological stance of peering through the multifaceted stained glass window, combined with the method of collecting 'stuff' in shoeboxes and the remarkable creativity of the young-people, provided a context for relaxed, sometimes humorous and sometimes emotive sharing of different viewpoints, knowledge, experiences, understanding and emotions. Individual objects sparked-off ideas between the young-people that led to wider evaluations of the topic and other stories being told beyond the remit of the initial object. This precipitated a continuous construction and re-construction of thoughts, and gave the conversations a dynamic quality. The sources, stories and scripts surrounding death in contemporary society, and the sights, sounds and silences associated with it were elegantly and eloquently explored within the context of their own thoughts, ideas and feelings. This uncovered their own contemporary landscapes of death, in which death existed in the reality of lived experiences, the fantasy of media sources and the internal landscapes of questions and reflections. The view through the window was indeed stunning.

In My Beginning Is My End

Death can be a bleak aspect of life to consider under any circumstances. I cannot contend that it is a discussion that old or young-people might want to engage in everyday, but there is a time and a place for most things, and perhaps we were lucky to find both. The conversations, and the stories told here illustrate how taking a look at death need not always be as austere, uninviting and forlorn as we might expect, indeed it can be engaging, evocative and insightful, perhaps even enjoyable. Mailer's essay, *The White Negro* (1957), considers death in the context of the horrors of World War II; concentration camps, atomic bombs and the fear, uncertainty and hopelessness this created for humanity. From such dreadful circumstances, Mailer argues, that a new and different type of person emerged, one who engaged with death and therefore life in innovative ways. These new interpreters of death were creative, rebellious, conforming, knowing, uncertain and pioneering. Surely, similar to these young-people and their perspectives on the end-of-life.

To conclude then, the conversations represented in this book have, however briefly, brought together the margins of youth and death through a belief in young-people as accomplished participants in research and as people who, like adults, have their own understandings of life and death. It has attempted to find a space in which the sociologies of death and childhood can combine to give a more effective and in-depth evaluation of how death is situated within ordinary everyday experiences. It has illustrated the ways in which death is a part of young-people's lives, their ability to talk about it and therefore what as adults we might hear, if only we choose to listen.

I contend that these young-people were the pioneers of this project, talking animatedly and in their own terms about the deaths they knew of and their own understandings of these. Some of these involved exploding in the air to save the world, some the sadness of loved ones who had died and therefore 'nothing is the same again', and some the love, romance and aesthetic beauty of undead vampires. Some included the existential musings of a life beyond death, or not. Some the longing to be remembered by others and some the anger felt at the treatment of a dying relative. One concerned the sight of his Grandfather's dead body, one to have her remains placed in a 'purple' box (her favourite colour) to be talked about long after her death, and one the invitation for us all to look at and touch death via the cremated remains of his Grandfather. Listening to these conversations has illuminated ordinary and everyday, yet thoughtful, insightful, and erudite worlds, in which death makes regular and often commonplace, entrances and exits into and out of the lives of young-people.

At the start of each conversation group, I asked if everyone was all right, if they were happy to go ahead and listen to, share and explore each other's stories, thoughts and ideas on the end-of-life. Amy (age 15), looking at her friends and inviting their response, commented …

Yeah it's ok. We're ok with death.

All her friends nodded in agreement.

References

Douglas, M. (1966/2002). *Purity and danger*. Abingdon: Routledge.

Elias, N. (1985). *The loneliness of the dying*. New York: Continuum.

Faulkner, J. (2008). The Innocence of victimhood versus the 'Innocence of Becoming': Nietzsche, 9/11, and the "Falling Man". *The Journal of Nietzsche Studies, 35*(36), 67–68.

Faulkner, J. (2011). *The importance of being innocent: Why we worry about children*. Port Melbourne: Cambridge University Press.

Fearnley, R. (2012). *Communicating with children when a parent is at the end-of-life*. London: Jessica Kingsley.

Kastenbaum, R., & Fox, L. (2007). Do imaginary companions die? An Exploratory Study. *Omega—Journal of Death and Dying, 56*(2), 123–152.

Maddrell, A., & Sidaway, J. D. (2010). *Deathscapes: Spaces for death, dying, mourning and remembrance*. Surrey: Ashgate.

Mailer, N. (1957). The white Negro, *Dissent*, Autumn. Retrieved April 14th 2013, from http://www.dissentmagazine.org/online_articles/the-white-negro-fall-1957.

McManus, R. (2013). *Death in a global age*. Basingstoke: Palgrave Macmillan.

Postman, N. (1982). *The disappearance of childhood*. New York: Vintage Books.

Ribbens McCarthy, J. (2006). *Young-people's experiences of loss and bereavement: Towards an interdisciplinary approach*. Berkshire: Open University Press.

Silverman, P. R. (2000). *Never too young to know*. Oxford: Oxford University Press.

Walter, T. (2008). The Presence of the Dead in Society, A paper presented at the conference on death and dying in 18–21c Europe, Alba Iulia, Romania. Retrieved July 22nd 2012, from http://www.bath.ac.uk/cdas/research/.

Index

© The Editor(s) (if applicable) and The Author(s) 2017
S. Coombs, *Young People's Perspectives on End-of-Life*,
Studies in Childhood and Youth, DOI 10.1007/978-3-319-53631-6

Printed by Printforce, the Netherlands